To Nicola
with love
Gran Grandma. x

'CATS' TALES'

or

'One Man and his Cats'

by

Tom Freeman-Keel

Best W

Tom Freeman-Keel

Supporting 'Cats Protection'

£1 goes to Cats Protection
for every book sold

'CATS' TALES' or 'One Man and his Cats'

Also by Tom Freeman-Keel
'From Auschwitz to Alderney and Beyond'
Plays
'September Story'
'New Lives for Old'
Poems
Short Stories

ISBN 0 9526 912-1--3

British Library cataloguing in Publication Data
A catalogue record for this book is available from the British Library

Published in 2000

Publisher's note: while every effort has been made to ensure that the information in this book is correct the Publishers do not accept responsibility for any inaccuracies.

To protect people's privacy some names have been changed.

Published by Seek Publishing, PO Box 3, Craven Arms, Shropshire SY7 0WB

Originated by MRM Graphics Ltd, Buckinghamshire, England
Printed in Singapore under the supervision of
MRM Graphics Ltd, Buckinghamshire, Engalnd

Contents

Note: Page numbers accompanying captions to the pictures indicate where the text relates to a picture.

An Endorsement by
Derek Conway TD
Chief Executive
CATS PROTECTION

Dear Reader
I am delighted to commend this work by Tom Freeman-Keel who's love of cats is apparent from every page of this remarkable book.

Tom's generous support towards our Cat Welfare Work is deeply appreciated and we wish him every success in this special venture.

Acknowledgements and Thanks

Where does one begin to say 'thank you' to all those friends, too numerous to mention here, for their help and encouragement in producing this book? At the beginning I suppose …

For the delightful photograph we have used for the front cover … acknowledgements to John Daniels. Then to Sophie Napier of Ardea who helped me negotiate its release.

Perhaps most important of all in the early days, my friend (now sadly deceased) Ramsey Ross who kept faith and gave me the results of his research.

Also, in the early days, to Linda Birch, Animal Artist for reading my manuscript and again in later days, Eileen Spencer Trott, who also read.

Then there were the folk who sent me photographs some of which I have used, and without which the book would lose some of its interest and amusement. In particular to Marianne, and Dennis Miller of Chelmsford, Geoff French of Yatton who sent his own personal picture of that incredible cat Pilsbury; the Rev. Stephen Cawley, Vicar of the Parishes, of Gwernaffield and Llanferras with his story of Tigger the pious cat; Scarlett Cliff for permitting the story of 'Minnie' the chimney sweep; Mr J. C. Parton for the use of his story about Tessie; Jamie Boness for permitting the story of Button who was buried alive; Mrs Chiu and her daughter Claire for the story of Barney and the washing machine.

Thanks too to my son Paul who said he didn't mind if I used his poem about 'Sootie'.

Thanks for permission to use stories in newspapers are due in particular to Sarah Jane Smith of the *Shropshire Star* who so generously gave access to a number of stories in the True Story Section; to the *Daily Mail*, the *Express*, the *Swindon Evening Advertiser* and other papers.

Very particular thanks are due to Mr Derek Conway, Chief Executive of Cats Protection for his cooperation and, encouragement; and finally to Miss A. E. Preston for her patience, encouragement, and coffees unlimited, whilst I wrote.

Tom Freeman-Keel

Introduction to 'CATS' TALES'

This is a book about cats for cat lovers and worshippers.

The cats in this book are not the tailor's dummies one finds in some cat books but real, ordinary cats, leading day to day lives and the stories are of the 'Yous' and the 'Mes' of the cat world.

They are the 'Coronation Streeters' and 'Eastenders' of the cat world and each had their own special personalities, their foibles, their weaknesses and strengths, mental and physical, and they, like you or me, reacted and adapted. to the environment and the circumstances of the moment and of the time in which they found themselves.

There is the aggressive neighbour; you will find the young one who gave the older one no peace; the pain and the bewilderment at the loss of a good friend and finding oneself alone; the happiness where one lived and being forced to move with all the traumas and anxieties which such moves bring; the getting to know a new area; the establishing oneself amongst the community and, perhaps, being exposed to the danger of traffic after the peaceful environment just left.

The fact that, except in narrative, there is little to be found in this book about the proper care and healthy feeding, grooming and breeding of cats is because there are already many excellent books on these subjects. This does not mean I do not recognise. the immense importance of the proper care and understanding of a cat, for only by loving care and understanding of a cat can you be sure YOUR cat will be happy and healthy.

Here and there the cat lover will find a comment or an observation on the life and behaviour of cats which I hope will stir happy memories and perhaps raise a new awareness of these wonderful animals.

Here and there too, I have permitted, myself the extravagance of making a reflective comparison of the character and behaviour of cats and humans.

I hope a shred of conscience will be stirred in those people who would turn their pet animals into toys or slaves or vehicles of commercial or prideful advantage, or worse still who simply look upon cats as useful vessels for experimental purposes.

Cats, like a golden thread have run through the fabric of my life and the stories which I tell will not, I hope, be labelled as 'anec-dotage', but accepted as a collection of reminiscences of a man whose turbulent life was made bearable and enriched by the company of the cats, who, from time to time, shared his adventures and his woes.

The stories in this book are of the stuff of living both for you, me and for our cats. They are *all* true.

Tom Freeman-Keel

Preface

For thousands of years cats were exalted to the most dignified positions in Society in civilisations as great as our own.

Over 2000 years ago cats were revered in India. They were adopted by Buddhists to guard their temples in Burma and a thousand years before that raised to the position of a God by the Egyptians.

Mankind, because he found he could not enslave the cat nor understand it, elevated it either to a position of great eminence or dressed it with a cloak of mystery or evil implications.

Is it a sign of the times when some Vets note down on their records 'CDC' (common domestic cat)? Is this a sign of a swing towards the Cat Fancier's wish that only (as in the USA) high bred ones are worthy of special mention and … ipso facto a general decline in attitude towards the 'ordinary' cat?.

There would seem to be no 'common domestic dog'. Dogs are identified by breed. (or the nearest) so why not cats in a similar way and by their markings?

* * *

Since civilisation began Mankind has found it necessary to place those things he could not tame or train, or did not understand into the categories of 'Good' or 'Evil'.

It was inevitable that the cat should be elevated to a symbol of 'Good' or 'Evil' thereby becoming representative of God or the Devil.

In some parts of the world black cats are considered unlucky but in Britain, tradition believes that providing they have six white hairs on their chest, they are lucky. White cats are considered lucky in other parts of the world. The cat, it seems, in one way or another achieves significance in the eye of Man.

The Black Cat serves as the Witch's companion, the Tabby Cat, with the mark of Merlin the Magician on his head, is especially favoured.

Yet religious sects have symbolised their antipathy towards one another, the Protestants and the Roman Catholic Churches, by burning the cat at the stake, confirming Man's resentful and reluctant respect, or fear, of the animal.

It seems that what Mankind fears, or cannot understand, or cannot control he must destroy.

Yet … is it not strange that a branch of the Cat Family … the Lion, should be called the 'King of Beasts'? Is it not, curious that the fastest animal on earth should be the Cheetah and the most feared and formidable animal of all should be the Tiger? Some would argue that the cat family is also the most graceful.

In India a few hundred years ago, despite regular devastation of the village populations, the Tiger was revered and rarely hunted. So big and powerful is the Tiger it can move a buffalo many times its own weight, on its own, a feat which it would take 13 strong men to achieve.

As civilisations and knowledge progressed the cat's position, in the Western World has declined but suspicions lingered on into the middle ages. 'Cat in the Bag' target practice was regular sport as was 'Swinging the Cat' in those days.

Is the society in which we live today more civilised than those of 1000 years and more ago? Whilst in those days the cat was considered to be either God or the Devil, the modern attitude of those who do not love or understand the cat is one of contempt or denigration, an attitude not far removed from days gone past.

It is not long ago that cats were listed as vermin in Britain. Cats do not have to be registered but dogs do, probably originating from days when dogs were the property of the favoured classes.

'If you cannot handle a situation, destroy it' is one of the most primitive reactions of Mankind and is as present today as ever before. It reaches deep down into our soul and emerges sometimes, as terrorism, vandalism and the illtreatment of cats.

So, if you would be happy, treat a cat with the respect it deserves. It may make a fool of you from time to time, but, it will never make a fool of itself.

Because a cat is so independent it will always have the upper hand … by understanding the cat we come to accept that fact and even, perhaps, ourselves.

Once you have acknowledged the cat for what it is, whether you are an ailurophile or an ailurophobe* you will be a happier person.

To those who are owned by a cat, whilst it sits on your lap or whilst you are opening the umpteenth tin of cat food. and it purrs and rubs against your legs, ponder on the thought … is the cat lover a cat lover because the cat symbolises the independence of thought and deed which we all secretly wish for?

Finally, a word of praise for vets, everywhere who keep our beloved pets healthy and happy, and who are, in my experience, not visited often enough or soon enough (in many cases) by many pet owners.

*See 'Cat-tionary' at end of book page 113.

Chapter One

TOMMY (NOVEMBER 1917)

I met Tigger at 3.30 pm on Tuesday December the 10th 1985.

With further acquaintance he proved to be one of the most intelligent and remarkable cats I have ever met. I feel qualified to make that observation because cats have been in my life, except for a few dismal years, for 76 years.

This book is a collection of stories about those cats, and as a consequence must inevitably contain snippets of my own life, for which I apologise.

If this were a recorded tape of past times you would be hearing the tap of my typewriter, and in the quietness as I pause to think, the sonorous deep snore of Tigger who was my faithful companion, and who would have been lying on the windowsill within two feet of me or sitting on the papers I was using.

But I digress, I lived with Tigger for many years and the rapport which seemed immediate upon us meeting one another developed into a deep friendship of mutual respect.

At least that is what I still like to think and remember.

When there is no cat in the house, or to be more precise, living with me with whom I can share the days events I experience an absence of fulfilment to my day. This has nothing to do with the quality and richness of my life at the time for however good that may be, there *must* be a cat.

Some cat lovers may disagree with me. Perhaps they have not achieved that deep common bond which I have found with a number of cats, not, let me hasten to add, *all* cats but a number.

I believe every cat even the stray 'moggie' has a personality of its own and like human beings, each one is different. Now and then in this book as a result of my observations of humans and their relations with animal I have offered a few ideas which may prove provocative.

Apart from all the cats with whom I have struck up a passing acquaintance … and I seem to do this at every street corner and everywhere I go … I realised recently that Tigger was the ninth cat in my life.

Cats are supposed to have nine lives – I wonder if there is anything significant in that?

Tommy

Old men are apt to dream of the past and their memories are supposed to be better for events which may or may not have happened 50 years ago than the present but I have to confess that my detailed recollections of Tommy are not as clear as I would wish.

Most of us have a few photographic image sharp memories of totally irrelevant events in our lives and I can remember a few related to Tommy.

It is sad to have to confess that I have no photographic record of Tommy. This probably because Tommy appeared in my life when we moved from a flat in Maida Vale in London to one of those tall Victorian houses in Bayswater.

I was six and World War One was coming to an end.

We had no cat then.

I jumped out of the removal van and sprained my ankle

On looking back it seemed a little strange that whilst we lived in a flat the family pet was a brindled Staffordshire Bull Terrier which bit me a couple of times. Probably because I teased it.

When we moved to the Bayswater house, 'Blackie' as he was inaccurately named, did not come with us. To my delight, and presumably as a replacement of 'Blackie', there appeared in no time at all a big ginger called 'Tommy'.

I was never sure who was responsible for bringing Tommy into the home. It may have been persuasion from my sister; certainly not my mother who had no particular fondness for any kind of animals. I think it was much more likely my father, who on one of his not infrequent bouts of inebriation was liable to bring home anything from a grand piano to a donkey and show it off with an air of dissembling pride and elan it was difficult to ignore or condemn.

So it was probably my father, in one of his moments of contrition who brought home Tommy.

Tommy (November 1917)

I had of course met cats before and like most children had delighted in their soft feel and the warmth of their fur. I was not wary of cats as I was of dogs.

It bothered me little, of course, at the age of six where this wonderful creature had come from. I suppose all I was aware of was that it certainly was not a dog and wasn't going to bite me.

Perhaps it was already accustomed to children for I recollect hugging it to me and finding a great comfort in its willingness to be fondled. I don't recollect that it purred but I'm sure it did.

I do remember that to me he seemed fully grown. He certainly was not a kitten. He was big and he was ginger.

Perhaps he was a replacement for the home troubles we were then going through and my father was perhaps cleverer than any of the family gave him credit for, in realising it would take my mind off less pleasant circumstances.

Perhaps therein … so a psychologist might try to explain … lies the need I feel for a cat in my life to come home to and to confide in.

Tommy and I were friends immediately.

I remember how impatient I became when he sat on the six foot high garden wall surveying everything around him with an imperious look and completely ignoring me.

Tommy was a big, heavy cat and the tops of the high brickwalls in those Victorian Bayswater gardens ware naturally out of my reach, but not so Tommy who seemed to be blessed with invisible wings which carried him effortlessly in one leap to the top of the wall.

We occupied the ground floor flat so had the use and responsibility of the gardens back and front and I have vague recollections of anxious discussions with my parents about the possibility of Tommy being run over or running away. An unnecessary concern, but an understandably childish one when one considers there were few cars in those days only horse drawn Lyons Bread carts and the like.

Tommy enjoyed the garden but like all cats was always around when food was being prepared. There was no canned cat food in those days, one went down the market and bought fish or some horse meat. When food was there so was Tommy rubbing against my legs, purring and nearly knocking me over. Tommy, who had his own cardboard box stuffed with newspapers, preferred to sleep with me, and got up to every kind of subterfuge to avoid being chased from my bedroom by my mother.

It need hardly be said Tommy had my full cooperation was my constant companion and I loved him.

I remember one occasion very vividly when Tommy did go missing. At the time I thought it was the end of the world.

Every year it was customary for us to have a fireworks and bonfire night party in the back garden and I recollect there was a pergola with a seat for three people on which had been laid out all the fireworks (that was silly for starters of course). Anyway they were, and it is not surprising, on reflection, that sooner or later on one of these evenings a spark from an ignited firework was going to set the whole lot off.

It happened.

The chaos, confusion, terror and excitement which ensued is not difficult to imagine. In an area which could not have been much larger than 30 feet by 60 feet, surrounded by high brick walls, with apart from escaping into the house or via a narrow gate both of which means of escape were close to the centre of the explosions, the guests were running around like rabbits.

There were chinese crackers, golden rain, bangers, aerial torpedoes and rockets and lots more with names I now cannot remember, all providing a most spectacular display, whistling, whizzing and banging in every direction, in an ever increasing kaleidoscopic cacophony of sound and colour.

No one had remembered to put Tommy safely away in a room before the evening began so that it was not until some time later someone said 'where's Tommy'. And so the search started with me becoming increasingly tearful and upset as we failed to find him.

I thought he had gone for ever. We went out into the street calling his name, my father climbed over the walls surrounding our garden and looked for him; we looked in all the rooms but there was no Tommy.

Then, when my parents were going to bed they glanced up to the top of the wardrobe and there was Tommy, safe but still nervous. I remember my father saying quite calmly he wouldn't have been surprised if he had found one of the guests up there with Tommy too.

Eventually of course, Tommy had to die. It was my first experience of someone close to me dying. I was distraught. For all my father's shortcomings I think he had a better understanding of my feelings than anyone else in the family.

Tommy was buried under a rose bush with great ceremony and I remember my father telling me that Tommy would still be helping us because the rose bush would grow better and give us more roses and that they would smell nicer.

There is of course one aspect of Tommy which I had almost forgotten yet it (perhaps I should say 'they') were the source of periodic friction between my parents and that was Tommy's private parts.

He was extremely well endowed. He had come to us not having been neutered and my father, demonstrating what one today might describe as masculine sympathy, argued that he was now too old for that operation. Anyway, they were the best and the largest pair he had ever seen and if Tommy was not aware of this, he, my father, was. This of course produced a barrage of scornful remarks from my mother which cannot be repeated here.

Like all toms Tommy sprayed and Tommy smelt. And Tommy's smell at certain times of the year was particularly obnoxious. Tommy should, of course, have been neutered at an early age.

By some miracle or perhaps a sense of respect for his own home Tommy rarely sprayed within the home but he *did* spray around the garden and sometimes near the outside lavatory. As my father remarked 'well, you can't expect him to use the seat!'

Many years of experience with cats has made me realise that Tommy was probably more of a character than I, in my childish innocence realised, for contrary to the behaviour of most undoctored toms who go seeking their affairs Tommy enticed his girl friends into his own backgarden (probably meowing his own version of 'come and see my etchings') with the result that we were frequently subjected to the serenades which accompany such nocturnal activities.

Am I imagining that after one of such disturbed nights he actually exaggerated the way in which he walked. He swaggered and showed off. Undoubtedly Tommy had a good life and he enriched ours. I sometimes wondered if my father was perhaps a little envious of Tommy.

As I remember it there was a gap of time before I obtained a cat of my own. It seemed a very long time but was no doubt only a matter of months.

Chapter Two

JENNIE, MAX AND JO

Jennie was delivered in a box. No one had bothered to puncture any air holes in the box and I remember my father complaining about this.

Jennie had belonged to my friend who's parents did not approve of pets in the home of any kind and Jennie had been permitted for a limited trial period only. It was luck for Jennie I was without a cat at the time otherwise, no doubt, she would have been 'put down'. My friend's parents were like that.

Poor Jennie. Looking back I suppose Jennie's lack lustre character was due simply to not having been wanted or loved, being as a result, poorly fed and ignored. She was a little ginger kitten with a sad expression and none of the exuberance and confidence of Tommy.

It seemed quite a long time before she began to put on weight and began to feel part of the family. But she always retained that slim figure and when I asked if she was going to have kittens I was told 'she can't … she's been to the Doctor…'

Despite her having been spayed we suffered the usual periodic visits from local toms at certain times of the year. Jennie began to run to me for protection but not before she had been involved in various attacks … one cannot use the word 'fights' for she did not fight back … and had her ear torn, face scratched and on one occasion a nasty cut on her leg which I personally tended, refusing to permit either my father or mother to assist me.

From then on Jennie refused to leave my side and the special feeling between us grew. I was teased by my sister who said 'she's not like poor old Tommy'. Well … she wasn't … but she was a cat and we had got to love one another and I enjoyed protecting her.

She was fussy about her food and seemed never, despite all our efforts to achieve that robust health which Tommy had enjoyed, to enjoy life.

Then, after a few years, Jennie who had been let out for her usual evening stroll did not return. It was winter, bitterly cold and snowing. We were particularly anxious because Jennie, as my mother used to say, 'had a weak chest'. Perhaps it was Jennie's vulnerability which brought out flickers of liking and concern in my mother which had never been present in her attitude towards Tommy.

After three days poor Jennie returned looking dreadful with her coat coagulated with mud, a tear in her face which was covered with blood and she was panting.

I insisted on going with my mother (strange that it was always my Mother who was supposed not to like animals, who rose to the occasion in times of crisis with our pets) to the Vets.

Jennie was stitched up and cleaned but she still seemed very ill. We took her home and coddled her but very gradually she went into a decline. Hers was not the natural death from old age like Tommy's … and I agonised on her behalf during the period up to her death. She was buried alongside of Tommy, who was making the roses grow very nicely.

I was now a latch-key student, my mother working part-time three or four days a week and it had been some time before I had acquired a replacement for Jennie. The many distractions of school and growing up softened the loss of Jennie but returning home after school to an empty house revived my need for companionship so I was allowed a cat.

Max

Why on earth we called him Max I just don't know. He was just out of kittenhood, neutered, house trained and a very ordinary looking tabbie of about average size, with absolutely nothing outstanding about him.

He had what we would refer to today as an air of being 'street wise'. Perhaps it was the life he led before he came to us and his very ordinariness which gave him this aura of self-sufficiency and assumed indifference to my loving, affectionate approach.

For all his assumed indifference Max, after living with us for a few weeks, began appearing when I got home from school.

This was not a question of waiting to be fed for he had access to the house at any time. He was not like Tommy nor like Jennie who, for their different reasons, came to me for love and to be stroked, in fact when I picked him up to cuddle him he struggled to be let down. It was sufficient for him to be somewhere near me with the option of walking out whenever he wished.

Because he had been neutered his negotiations with the opposite sex were of course limited although his imagination must, at times, have been very vivid. He seemed to avoid the usual fights with the other toms in the area, who were mistakenly wary of him as he sat in his usual position dead centre of the high wall at the end of the garden, looking far more self-possessed and aggressive then he really was.

It was in this position, sitting bolt upright, with tail drooping down over the edge of the wall, front legs and paws close together, I remember him most clearly.

He was always clean of course, yet poor Max, whatever he did and however hard he tried, his very colouring and his coat, always gave him the appearance of being untidy and needing a wash.

It was much much later in life when I thought about him and about people I noticed that there were people who suffered the same misfortune, of, despite their efforts, looking 'drab'.

What a gamble life is when one realises that much of the happiness, the success or the failure which befalls us is determined by the way we look! And animals, all animals, are the same, particularly domesticated animals such as cats, dogs, horses etc.

Have you ever visited an R.S.P.C.A. establishment where there are cats and dogs waiting to be chosen by would be pet owners? Watch and listen, as they pass from one cage to another. 'He looks a bit fierce'; 'He's too big'; 'He will eat too much'; 'Oh! isn't she beautiful!; 'I love her colouring'; 'Now *He's* handsome!' 'Just look at those lovely sad eyes!'; and so on.

Are we obliged to admit that it is the trivialities of life which determine our future?

And so Max lived on with us for many many years. He never, as Tommy had done, became an intimate member of the family. My sister, who was six years older than me, had her own special room and I seem to remember Max spent more time with her than he did with me, that is, until she left home to marry, when I took over her room.

Max visited me then. I now wonder if it was the room he liked and not the occupant!

When Max died of old age I buried him near, but not with, Tommy and Jennie, which is some indication that even if you have done no harm in your life if you haven't got the right charisma you are not buried in St. Pauls Cathedral or Westminster Abbey!

Not long after I had buried Max we moved to what we used to call 'the family house'. It was not far away. It was also on a busy road junction. The front door was on the pavement. My need for a cat in my life seemed less imperative because I was soon away to work in the Midlands for a few years where I stayed in a boarding house.

So the boarding house cat and I soon became the best of friends and Mrs Grimshaw, the Boarding House proprietoress could hardly believe I was sincere when I asked her to leave my room door open in order that Jo, who was a smooth haired black neutered tom should have access to sleep on my bed.

He was there, without fail, every evening when I returned from work only returning periodically to his mistresses' apartment to be fed. Whilst Mrs Grimshaw pretended to be amused she was obviously vexed about Jo's infidelity and Jo cost me many a box of chocolates to keep the lady 'sweet'.

In the intervening years leading up to outbreak of war I was too often away to conscientiously have a cat, and when I joined up, I was glad I was not obliged to ask my parents to look after a cat for me whilst I was away.

Cats in India and Burma

I was amongst the first contingent when war was declared to be sent to India and Burma.

When we arrived there were already plenty within the existing army camps of the established Indian Army of both dogs and cats and in the more remote army establishments the domestic animals were constantly under attack from groups of wild and semi-wild dogs which ranged around the perimeters of the camps especially on the North West Frontier. I did notice however, throughout India, there were far less numbers of cats than what I had expected.

Wild cats were most prevalent around the villages of the Punjab. They were almost totally nocturnal and the natives were unbelieving when I told them we had cats as pets in England, although of course the Indians working in the Army camps were well aware of this. To many Indian villagers cats were a menace and a danger.

In the fabulous palace of the Maharajah of Jodhpur where I spent a few days there was not a cat to be seen, although 2000 years ago as part of their culture they were revered as demi-gods.

What is it about the British I wondered, that gives them this special interest and concern about animals which, I venture to suggest, is not to be found to the same degree in any other nationality in the world?

Chapter Three

BUTCH AND THE HOME COMING

I returned home to live in the house in which I had been born, the same house where I had moved before the outbreak of war. I had been away almost six years. My father had died and my mother had become very frail. There was no cat to welcome me.

Soon I was alone in the house for my mother had gone to live with my sister. Within a year or so I married and my wife came to live with me in the 'family house'.

As I remember it we met because we had been standing outside a pet shop watching some kittens for sale in the window. You know how such things begin … I say 'you seem very fond of cats' … she says 'I love all animals but particularly cats' … I say 'do you have any now?' She says … 'No, sadly not, do you?' … I say 'no! I've not long been back from abroad' … 'I'm reorientating' … 'would you like a coffee?' … She says 'yes, we can talk about cats'. And that is how it all began.

My job took me away for days on end sometimes and it was during one of my absences our permanent guest arrived. Phoning home one evening as was my habit when away my wife said 'Oh! by the way we've got a guest staying with us, I hope you don't mind!' … 'He's a 'he'.' I said 'well if he's one of your old boy-friends he'd better be gone by the time I get back'. She said 'Darling, don't be silly, he's a cat! And with the word 'cat' the clouds lifted from me and I simply said 'keep him'.

When I got home and met 'him' I began to think I had, perhaps, been a little rash for 'he' was not as I had imagined 'him'.

My wife had already named him and a very appropriate name I thought it was too. She had called him 'Butch'. Butch was already well established by the time I arrived. He had chosen his favourite chair and decided where he would sleep at nights.

Apparently, my wife told me, she had left the door open one day and in had walked Butch. He had walked straight past my wife without so much as an acknowledgement and settled down in front of the fire, having first inspected the place to see if it was to his liking.

Butch was one of the biggest ginger neutered toms I had ever seen . I have only once seen a bigger cat. As my wife remarked on my return home and we sat looking at Butch reclining in my favourite chair 'he doesn't seem to be over fussy about his appearance but perhaps we can change that'. I said 'don't you think he's a bit too old to change his ways?'. She said 'is that a hint you are giving me about yourself?'.

I said, in a clumsy attempt to change the subject, 'You know, I think that remark of yours about Butch must have been more in hope than intent'.

Butch, as you will guess, remained in appearance much the same as he had arrived despite all our efforts.

Butch was already some years old when he adopted us. He was, or had been, obviously a fighter, for he was already scarred from many battles. He had a pale ginger coat with the slightest of faint white stripes running from the centre of his back down either side to an almost white tummy. He had white feet, which were huge.

My wife said when I was away she looked at Butch's feet and thought of me, not because they were white but because they were big for I took a size 12.

What made Butch look even bigger was his coat which was not really a pure short hair in density or length and so he seemed always to look untidy, except I must say, his feet, which, if no other part of him, he kept immaculate.

I reminded my wife that my father had told me 'even if your clothes *are* old, you can go anywhere providing your clothes are brushed and your shoes are clean'.

Butch had a big head too but his eyes and his ears seemed too small to match the rest of him. As with some big fat men his voice seemed too small for him for his 'meow' was unpredictable sometimes eminating as a well rounded sound and at other times being nothing more than a squeak. Butch seemed as surprised as we were when a 'little noise' as wife called it was all he could manage.

To offset his lack of beauty Butch was intelligent, he knew precisely what he wanted at all times, which was, as my wife pointed out, more than could be said of me.

He was niggardly with his affections doling them out with an air of regality, like a Monarch on Maunday Thursday giving out the monies to the poor. I argued he behaved like this because he was clever enough to know that the more aloof he was the more we pandered to him. He ran the house and the house was run around him and had there arisen the question of who should stay and who should leave, he or we, I feel it is we who would have left.

There was no doubt that Butch was a fighter for he had no sooner established his residential rights within the house than he began to mark out his territory around the house.

There were a few battles from which he emerged unscarred after which there was no doubt the gardens back and front were his domain including the surrounding walls upon which he spent hours surveying his realm. His manner and the area which he vigorously defended were not dissimilar from that which I remembered Tommy holding court in and I confess my memories of the two cats, because of this, are somewhat confused.

If I was not away on a business trip then I went to the City daily and I was assured by my wife that Butch always knew if I was coming home. He didn't bother, if I wasn't coming home that evening, to make the circuitous route necessary across gardens and gaps in order to sit on the garden wall where he would normally greet me.

Butch knew my movements as well as I did myself.

He knew if I was to be away for the day or if I was just going out for half an hour. If the latter then he wouldn't move from his slumbers but if it was 'hat, briefcase and umbrella' he was up and rubbing his great big ginger bulk against my legs, and walking with his big paws all over my shoes as if trying to prevent me from leaving.

My wife and I enjoyed classical music and it was fortunate that Butch too also enjoyed it although he made it quite apparent his approval of our taste was limited to the better known and older composers. He did *not* like Stravinsky, Shostakovich or Tippett and raised his head with an expression of doubt on his face when we played Sibelius.

Around this time Uncle Harry, who lived alone and who was lonely, took to calling upon us. He was passionately fond of music and enjoyed the evenings when we played some of his favourite composers.

Unhappily for Uncle Harry he hated cats and, as is the way of cats, Butch insisted on making a fuss of him. I'm sure Butch took a sadistic delight in approaching Uncle Harry in a menacing way. Whenever Butch did this Uncle Harry froze and there was no doubt Uncle Harry's enjoyment of the music was badly impaired when Butch leapt lightly on to his lap and settled down purring.

Uncle Harry was too terrified to push him off and would sit there stiffly like a dummy not daring to move. There were times when I could swear Butch looked at us and winked as much as to say 'we'll soon get rid of him' and I must confess there were times when Uncle Harry's visits were not convenient. On these occasions we left Butch on Uncle Harry's lap knowing it would not be long before he decided to leave. If we were happy to have his company for the evening Butch would be persuaded to leave Uncle Harry alone.

It was a coincidence that Uncle Harry particularly enjoyed Sibelius the composer which caused Butch to raise his head and complain. My wife seemed to take a sadistic delight in waiting for Butch to settle on Uncle Harry's lap and then to play something by Sibelius. Butch's immediate reaction was to sit up look straight in Uncle Harry's face and give a short sharp little yelp. Uncle Harry was so terrified when this happened I had to persuade my wife from playing this little trick in case he had a heart attack.

Very gradually Uncle Harry got used to Butch and when Butch finally died Uncle Harry seemed almost as upset as we were.

Whilst the front door of the house was on the pavement it gave access to a reception area built on the front of the house. The roof of the reception area had been transformed into a balcony, or verandah, at first floor level and it was not uncommon for Butch to be seen sitting on the balcony wall waiting my return home and looking like one of those stone lions one often sees at entrances to large estates.

It was, I suppose, inevitable with the front door on the pavement and our gardens only yards from a busy road that poor Butch should be run over.

He had, during the few years he had spent with us, not only endeared himself to us but to the community around. He had become a respected personality not only in his own world of cats but amongst the humans too.

There was a public house not far away from us and I well remember one day seeing a much inebriated gentleman, unsteady on his feet, holding a very serious conversation with Butch, who was sitting in his accustomed place on the wall, looking at his friend in a most disapproving way as he had a finger waved in his face.

He was brought to us with reverence one morning lying across the outstretched arms of a tearful Sikh who ran the corner shop a few hundred yards away.

He had been hit by a car. He was dead.

That night my wife and I got rather drunk as we listened to Chopin's Funeral March Sonata the second movement of which had us in floods of tears.

It seemed that dear old Butch had sensed it was time for him to make his exit. We were planning to move 25 miles outside London into semi-country so that the baby, when it arrived, would be in a better environment.

As you have gathered … my wife was pregnant.

Chapter Four

SOOTIE … A CAT IN THE COUNTRY

Soon after the arrival of Paul we moved, as we had intended, into the country. No new cat had entered our lives which were full. A son, a new house and my job took up all our time to say nothing of making new acquaintances.

Establishing ourselves in a new environment, with me commuting to London, used up a lot of time and whilst we discussed the need for children to quickly become accustomed to animals, for the first year or so we did not acquire one.

Nevertheless it was with little surprise one day on returning home from work I was introduced to Miss Sooty Parker.

A friend, who apparently had already deduced we were cat lovers, had arrived with a grown kitten which needed a home.

It is I suppose the pressures of the surrounding environment that provoke the different attitude towards cats and amongst different levels of society.

Farm cats are more or less left to fend for themselves and generally, seem to do so perfectly adequately. Ships cats too have an instinct for survival, as also do cats associated with industrial areas in factories whilst there are probably more cats to be found in poorer districts than dogs. They are cheaper to feed and don't take up so much room in the home. They also keep down the mice one hopes.

In the better off country homes the cat, seems to take second place to the dog. Whilst the pampered cat is frequently found in the homes of rich widows and amongst the flat dwellers in the big cities. One wonders in which of these different situations a cat is happiest. Perhaps, like many humans if you don't know any different then you are likely to be content with your lot, and the nearer to one's natural instincts the more this is likely to be so. (see Tailpiece)

If the reasoning is correct then ipso-facto the farm cat is the happiest. But none of these things were taken into consideration when we acquired Miss Sooty Parker.

One of the little fascinations of my wife was her propensity to 'spoonerise' and whilst it was acceptable that our new and delightful acquisition should be introduced as Miss Sooty Parker, I must confess to some confusion on occasion to hear this mischevious bundle of black fur referred to as Miss Pooky Sorter.

Whilst it confused me it seemed perfectly reasonable to the childish mind of Paul. I was assured this was a perfectly reasonable transmutation, as the name, once one had understood the reason for the original name, described the insatiable curiosity of Sooty perfectly. There seemed little doubt that the least confused of the four of us was Miss Parker herself.

'Sooty' because she was black, was understandable, and 'Parker' because she was nosy, was acceptable. But 'Miss Pooky Sorter'!

When I queried this the slick explanation offered was 'Oh! but its simple ...'pooky' is the same as 'nosy' ... she 'pooks' into things and 'sorter' because she's kind of special'.

I recollect a friend of ours saying to my wife 'Damn it woman the poor animal doesn't know whether its 2 o'clock or Thursday'. I must confess that I cannot remember Miss Parker ever responding to the name of Miss Pooky Sorter.

A lively discussion ensued about the tendency for cats, not dogs, to be given various names and this was strongly defended by my wife. In the years since then it is a question which I have never heard argued convincingly until quite recently.

But my wife remained adamant in arguing that providing the *sound* is right a cat will respond to almost any similar sounding word. 'Tigger', 'bigger', 'snigger' ... all will do she argued.

I argue that this is a denigration of the cat's intelligence but Tigger's mistress says 'no'. But we will return to that later, this narrative is about Miss Sooty Parker.

Sooty Parker's crazy antics of jumping from one high place to another, trying to emulate a monkey as Paul said, and the way she ran up the trunk of the pear tree in our front garden was a source of never ending delight to

Paul. It seemed that Miss Parker knew this and deliberately put on a performance for Paul whenever he was around.

She seemed always to be sitting on something high above us. On top of a bookcase or a wardrobe or the kitchen cupboard, up a tree or on a wall and sometimes on the bungalow roof.

Her most amusing and favourite trick, at least from the point of view of my wife and myself was to sit gracefully upon the summit of one of the entrance gate posts to the bungalow.

Walking down the pathway to the gate, inexperienced visitors would almost all involuntarily exclaim 'Oh! isn't she pretty!', 'What a *delightful* little pussy'. One could almost see Miss Sooty Parker cringe at being called a 'pussy'. An almost imperceptible flick of the tail and we knew what was going to happen next. As the visitor passed beside and beneath the gate post there was a flash of a black paw and anyone wearing a hat would be wearing it no longer.

This happened over and over again until to watch and wait for it became a mesmeric fascination for both of us. If Paul was with us he joined in the fun but the great difficulty was to cover up his anticipatory giggles before it had happened.

If it was a friend we didn't really like – and you know what I mean by *that* one of us would stand in the gateway thus obliging the visitor to pass beneath and in reach of Miss Sooty Parker's lethal paw.

Miss Sooty Parker did for us what we would love to have done ourselves had we had the courage. Of course we were always *full* of apologies for the behaviour of such a *naughty* little cat 'and really we can't think *what* came over her'.

Miss Sooty Parker knew her reward would be a dish of her *very* favourite food when the visitors had gone.

Miss Sooty Parker was small, slim, young and lithesome. The sort of young lady old men dream about in their dotage. With apparently very little effort she kept herself quite immaculate. Her coat shone and glistened and was always in perfect order. She sat upright with her two front legs tightly together and her head carried primly on a long neck.

It was a habit of hers to leave her mouth ever so slightly open with the minute tip of a very pink tongue showing. She was a very provocative lady and had she been human would undoubtedly have worn nothing but the best of perfumes and high heels.

Even her speech (sorry … you *do* understand how it gets you, I hope) even her meows were 'better class' being short, sharp and quite distinct. She had of course been spayed but the respectful interest shown in her by the male cats of the district was remarkable. She accepted all of it as if it was her due.

As for me, my advances were accepted with a condescension and air of expectation which said 'you are OK but keep your distance' … 'I like you but that is no reason to be silly about it' … all of which only provoked me into behaving in an even sillier manner until my wife would say '*really* Tom!', and Paul, with his head on one side and a worried frown upon his face would say 'why do you do that Daddy?'.

After a year or so we moved to a more spacious house on the main road.* The gardens back and front were larger but Miss Parker missed the adjacent fields which had surrounded the bungalow. Being on the main road we worried that in this new situation she would be run over.

Within a matter of weeks we noticed a change in Miss Parker's behaviour. From a cat which explored everything within sight she became nervous refused to enter one of the smaller upstairs rooms and took to sleeping on our bed at every available opportunity.

She now scratched on the bedroom door and insisted on sleeping on the bed with us.

Her need for loving could not be ignored and she followed us about from room to room for company.

Then, one evening, my wife and I were sitting talking. Miss Parker was sitting on the arm of one of the armchairs, facing the door to the hall which was open.

Almost simultaneously my wife and I saw Miss Parker rise slowly to stand with arched back and fur erect. Her tail began to lash and she opened her mouth making little keening noises as cats do when watching birds.

We looked to the hall to see a ghostly figure gliding down the stairs. A short man in a raincoat … a Colombo mac. The ghostly figure paused at the bottom of the stairs and than melted away.

*See picture on page 128.

By this time Miss Parker had jumped down from her perch and was hiding behind the chair, fur still erect. The atmosphere it left behind was not pleasant. The temperature had dropped noticeably.

That visualisation was not the last we were to experience.

On returning from work one dark evening I found my wife in her outdoor coat, Miss Parker in her arms, in a state of almost hysteria. She had been out visiting friends and returned to meet the spectre in the hall.

From then on it was 'we must move... I won't stay in this place any longer'.

On mentioning the reason for our move to the Estate Agent he was not surprised. Apparently the house had a long history of disaster for its occupants. We were not the first to see the apparition.

So we moved to a house on stilts beside the river a few miles away. Almost next door to us was a boatyard. Miss Parker rapidly regained confidence and was frequently found wandering amongst the luxurious motor launches. Undoubtedly she enjoyed the atmosphere created by such better class activities, and the people there who made a fuss of her. Or was it the mice and the rats whhich abounded?.

She would gaze with fascination at her reflection in the still waters from the jetty at the bottom of our garden for hours and when she grew bored with this stalked off to the boatyard for company and excitement.

We had not been in this delightful spot long before my wife and I decided we should divorce. Had the haunted house once more done its work?

When we parted Paul went with my wife to live with her mother and took Miss Sooty Parker. For a period of time I was of 'no fixed abode ' and there was no opportunity to acquire a replacement to Miss Parker.

I was kept regularly informed of Paul's welfare and eventually he was sent to a Prep School. My ex-wife went to live on board a yacht with another gentleman where I was assured on enquiry that Miss Sooty Parker had taken to living on board 'like a duck takes to water'.

This might have been a little too literal and premature for I understood she eventually fell in and was drowned. As I afterwards remarked no one had told her she was not a duck!

I pondered at the time that perhaps Miss Parker had gazed at her reflection in the waters for too long, leaned over too far and fallen in. Do I detect a similarity with some ladies looking too long and too often in their mirrors?

It was later I was to learn that, like me, when I was beset by troubles, Paul too found his solace in his communion with a cat so the loss of Miss Parker –Paul's first cat–was greater for him than for any of us.

It was 23 years later when I again met his mother that I was shown a poem Paul had written about Miss Sooty Parker, or, as she was more fondly called by Paul–'Sootie'.

Here it is–Paul was 14 when he wrote it.

SOOTIE

Was ever such a pet so loved
As was my own who
Seeming not her furry self but human
Would both talk and mew?

Has ever such a pet since her so walked
As in a dream or played
So youthfully as she, who through our gate
Into our hearts once strayed?

I was too young to memorise that face,
so memorable now.
She was my age, and being thus I missed
her last meows.

That such a creature beautiful and lithe,
should in reality
Be dead, I could not grasp. I, young, gasped
and prayed her immortality.

It is too late to say 'Goodnight. goodbye'
My last farewells;
For she is dead, and in eternal bliss
In heaven, there she dwells.

I must say having read the poem, I wondered if my son had been feeling and responding as I had done when very young. Had taken refuge from a difficult world by creating his own, populated by those with whom he could communicate.

Do *all* children do this I wondered? Do parents take sufficient cognisance of each child's secret world? And ... does every animal have its own secret world too?

Chapter Five

CAT-CAT IN JERSEY, THE CHANNEL ISLANDS

It was a year or two before I once again dared to seek happiness through the companionship of a lady.

The two years leading up to our marriage were tumultuous; full of every kind of emotion from elation to total despair and through this period, as I was still of 'no fixed abode' had no opportunity to acquire a cat with whom I could discuss my problems.

When I did marry again I was fortunate to have found a lady who loved cats equally as much as I did but by then I was on a career course and starting a new life in a new home. The motivation and the need for a cat was not strong, there were other distractions too, such as being away from home for long periods and it was not until we moved to Jersey in the Channel Islands we again acquired a cat, for my new wife had missed *her* cat as much as I had missed mine.

In moving to Jersey I had decided to give up my career job, move to Jersey and start a business there. It was an adventure and we were fortunate in living in a choice spot on the cliff top overlooking St. Brelade's Bay.

Once again it was a cat who decided to adopt us.

The grounds surrounding the houses were spacious and so we were unaware of the dramatic proceedings in the big house to our left. We thought the French wife and the English husband were a happily married couple. They had two dogs and a cat and we saw all of them, dogs, cat and neighbours only occasionally.

One day we were intrigued to hear that what had, we were told, been a stormy marriage had finally disintegrated. They had left overnight taking the dogs and leaving instructions for the disposal of the contents but *not* so we discovered, the cat.

We had learned in earlier conversation with them that the cat had belonged to the wife and so it was therefore a French cat.

As you might well guess it was not long before La Petite Chatte as my wife immediately called her, had introduced herself and declared her intention to live with us. Apparently La Petite Chatte bore no malice towards her recent ex-master and mistress and with a true gallic shrug of the shoulders had turned her back on the house and come to live with us.

It seemed that I was destined to be blessed with women who had the enchanting ability to create amusing and fascinating names for people, animals and things and it was no time at all before La Petite Chatte had become 'Chat-Chat' because she talked a lot.

My wife so called her that because in the experiences of both of us she was the chattiest cat either of us had ever known. We were of course aware that she had come from Brittany and 'Chatte Chatte' very soon became translated into the English 'Cat-Cat'. It all seemed very obvious.

Cat-Cat was slim, sleek shiny and black and walked with the elegance and grace of a true French Lady of the Courts. As my wife remarked 'every Frenchwoman has a "little black number" in her wardrobe and this one seems to wear hers all the time'. Cat-Cat took great pride in her appearance and spent a great deal of time grooming herself. The activity which followed one of her fastidious meals had to be seen to be believed.

The elegant raise of the paw which was carefully brought down across from her forehead to the side of her mouth was a fascination. One wondered if she was ever going to finish in time for the next meal. She very rarely got herself dirty by rolling in the dust or squeezing into odd corners to satisfy her curiosity. One never saw her cleaning those parts of her which cats always seen so interested in and one wondered if, like the gentry, she ever went to the loo at all. Certainly one never saw her. She's a 'fairy' said my wife one day.

The relationship between Cat-Cat and myself was on an equally genteel footing. Certainly she was more 'giving' in her responses to me than Miss Sooty Parker had been and this rather surprised me. Perhaps she sensed in me the concern I felt for her and that admiration I had for her after her disgraceful abandonment by her previous master and mistress.

I was allowed so much of her company on my lap and if I was sitting on a bench in the garden she would sit beside me facing in the opposite direction to that which I was as if we were sharing one of those 'S' shaped Regency conversation chairs.

What delighted me was the almost measured amount of affection which Cat-Cat gave to my wife and myself although I was always convinced that the rapport which existed between Cat-Cat and my wife was much deeper than that between myself and her.

Like most animals Cat-Cat was jealous of her territory and ensured that no other cat or dog should invade it. She was a fiery little minx when dealing with other animals and it was with some alarm we found her facing up to a very large rat which had strayed into the garden.

There they were facing up to one another, sitting bolt upright on their haunches, having what passed very fairly for a boxing match. There was, as we watched, a great deal of cautious manoeuvring then suddenly almost too quick to be seen there were a few lightening flicks with her paw and the rat had had enough.

Cat-Cat preened herself with a few delicate licks to her paw and hardly ruffled fur and then stalked off tail high in the air. Had she turned as she passed us and said in French 'thats the last we shall see of *him*' I would not have been surprised. It was in fact one of the few times when she didn't say anything.

Cat-Cat or Chatte-Chatte had been well named for she never stopped talking, from which we concluded there must have been a streak of Burmese or Siamese in her pedigree.

The Cat lover will I am sure know what I mean when I try to describe a non-meow. It is not a grunt it is not a squeak, it is not a gentle growl and it is extremely difficult if not impossible for humans to copy it.

It is perhaps a little like the 'keening' noise a troubled dog will make and the best way I can describe or suggest to a human to copy it is by keeping the mouth closed and bringing air to the roof of the mouth through the throat.

The noise made by Cat-Cat could be conversational, or it could be demanding, it could also demonstrate contentment.

When we came home from work the greeting was noisy with hardly a pause for breath between one meow and the next and she danced around our legs so rapidly it was difficult to make progress.

We had been in Jersey almost three years when we decided to move to Guernsey joining business forces with an old friend of mine.

Throughout the day preceding our departure and most of the night there had been a frightful storm. As we were moving home everything we possessed, our home,, our car was on the boat at anchor in St. Helier Harbour to take us the 30 odd miles to Guernsey. As we looked across the bay and saw the wave heights we took it for granted we would not be sailing.

We had prevailed upon the hotelier to permit us to keep Cat-Cat in her cat box in the room with us. She had behaved impeccably. In fact, we had taken her down into the bar where an enchanted barmaid had provided her with milk. In her usual inimitable style she had washed herself and it was with great difficulty I managed to persuade the rest of the people in the bar not to open a bottle of champagne for toasting her and to see if she would drink it. As one more astute holidaymaker commented 'caviar would be more to her taste!'

So there we were next morning poised to board the boat. A boat which, not only contained our home and our car, but our business documents, our hopes, our aspirations and Cat-Cat was going to be on that boat too. To say we were apprehensive was an understatement for we had been made aware that there had been some differences of opinion as to whether departure should be delayed until the seas had quietened.

As we left harbour and proceeded to make that infamous crossing between the two islands the waves became higher and the bow and the stern of the ship took it in turns to point heavenward. When the stern left the water there was a frightening thunderous whirring swishing noise from the freed propellers.

One place not to be on a crossing like that is inside the ship. We had taken Cat-Cat with us of course in her box. People were being ill all over the place and the smell, to greatly understate it, was most unpleasant, so we took Cat-Cat in her box outside on the deck.

For the first time we were to see poor little Cat-Cat loose her poise. Between protesting vociferously she was being sick. In the confines of the box it was the first time we had seen her in such a state and we could do nothing to help her. It was as much as we could do to cling with both arms to an upright and keep the cat box from sliding all over the deck with our feet.

There was one heartstopping moment when the cat box escaped from between our feet and we thought it would slide overboard.

Poor Cat-Cat was very ill and slowly her noisy complaints subsided into a whimper. I felt it was as much from a feeling of degradation which upset her as the actual illness.

I must say that neither of us had realised a cat could be sea-sick and to see our elegant La Petite Chatte in such a state tore at our hearts.

The fright we had experienced when the cat box slid away was as nothing to what happened next. We nearly lost her overboard.

I could no longer bear seeing her in such a mess and made my way to the newspaper stand to obtain a clean base for her to lie on. It was closed of course but I managed to get them to give me what I wanted. I struggled back and we opened the box. Whilst I cleared the box out and put in clean paper my wife held Cat-Cat. Whilst she was doing so an unexpected lurch almost forced my wife to let go of Cat-Cat. My wife clung to her with one hand and with the other spun around the pole she was holding on to, whilst I went sliding down the deck with my hand inside the mucky cat box.

As I lay on my stomach on the wet deck one hand in the box the other clinging to a rail I watched Cat-Cat wriggling furiously in my wife's arm and gradually slipping out of her grasp. Both my wife and I realised in a flash that if once Cat-Cat was free she would be overboard. I also realised at the same moment that if my wife let go her hold on the pole, which was keeping her upright, to save Cat-Cat they would *both* be overboard. With an effort I released my hand from the cat box, scrambled to my feet and lurched across the deck to my wife just in time to restore her hold on Cat-Cat.

I then turned to recover the cat box which had been sliding about the deck, emptied it of the mucky paper and stuffed some clean inside quickly pushing a protesting and terrified Cat-Cat unceremoniously inside.

It was then, with some sanity restored that my wife burst out laughing, pointed at me and said 'just *look* at you'.

Eventually it was over, we had landed and we were installed in a delightful cottage we were to occupy for three months.

Cat-Cat recovered quickly and soon came to enjoy her new surroundings apart from being persecuted by a randy old ginger tom in whom she showed not the slightest interest.

My wife came to the conclusion he couldn't speak French and so Cat-Cat didn't understand what it was all about. I argued it was a universal language that knew no barriers and was surprised he had taken the trouble to introduce himself.

Within three months we had moved to the Pub which we had come to Guernsey to take over. It was a big one and we had a large and beautiful penthouse flat on the top floor.

Cat-Cat loved the roof garden scaring us stiff with her antics on the walls 40 feet above ground and looking around with disdain when we called her knowing I was too scared to get near the edge to fetch her back.

She spent long hours by herself, for as everyone knows, running a pub is demanding of one's time. I think she missed us for her welcome when we went to the flat late at night was more enthusiastic and noisier than ever.

She allowed us only a short period of relaxation before the clamour for further attention began again and could not be ignored.

For her, the change from the big garden and the cliffs of our Jersey house to the constriction of the flat and the roof garden with little happening must have been difficult to adapt to so we did our best to make it up to her by a period of play each night.

As everyone who has lived with a cat knows late at night is the time when cats come alive and most like to play. Cat-Cat was no exception and quite quickly a routine developed.

Her favourite game was hide and seek played from room to room along a very long passage with my wife hiding in one room and calling her name.

Cat-Cat would scamper from room to room pretending, when 'discovered' by one of us to be surprised, stopping in her progress with tail stiff and upright, back arched and all four legs spread akimbo Then, a leap into the air and she was rushing off only to go through the whole pantomime again.

This went on all the way down the passage until my wife was 'cornered' in the end room by Cat-Cat who was then rewarded with a hug (which I'm never quite sure whether she liked or not) and some chocolate dog biscuits which we had discovered she considered a delicacy.

The interesting part of all this was the way in which Cat-Cat retained her dignity and our respect.

Before we had moved to Guernsey Cat-Cat had already demonstrated her indifference towards people. When we held a party Cat-Cat would retire to some quiet spot in the house or garden and remain there until everyone had gone. It was probably the only time she was quiet. It did not surprise us therefore when she followed the same pattern in the pub. Cat-Cat rarely came down into the bars preferring her home and her gardens.

She must have been lonely for the rapturous greetings she afforded us were not reserved for our arrival late at night but occurred each time we entered the flat.

In little more than a year we decided to move back to 'the mainland' as Island people referred to it. Whether it was just the excitement of packing yet again, the empty boxes to play in and the packing material to hide in and scuff up or the fact that we were moving from a place in which she had not been too happy, I do not know. But certainly the moving preparations did not upset Cat-Cat, and more than once we had to rescue her from being sealed up in a packing case.

This time, we had decided, we would not subject Cat-Cat to the horrors of a sea trip, especially not one of so many hours. We obtained permission to take her by air and because we knew the crew, succeeded in persuading them to allow us to take her in the cabin.

Had we wanted to carry out this operation secretly we would have been discovered immediately for Cat-Cat was loud in her protestations once in the cat box. Was she remembering the sea-trip we wondered?

We had obtained seats right up front so that the cat box did not obstruct the passageway. Cat-Cat could see everyone and nearly everyone could see Cat-Cat. Everyone was talking about her and whenever a Steward passed the box he or she stopped to talk to her.

Cat-Cat's meows rose to a new crescendo as we took off subsiding to a regular short plaintive meow as we levelled off. There was no doubt she was not happy and I noticed that she had wet her paper padding and was uncomfortable. There was nothing I could do about that until we had landed.

We had about us one or two items which we were uncertain whether we should declare or not including the rather nice fur coat worn by my wife.

As we walked out of the plane and across the tarmac towards Customs my wife nudged me, took the basket from my hand and said 'leave this to me'. Then followed a most remarkable performance both by Cat-Cat and my wife.

If someone had afterwards told me my wife had secretly rehearsed Cat-Cat how to behave on arrival at Customs I would not have been surprised for she suddenly set up the loudest session of howling, yeowling and meowing I had yet heard.

Immediately, my wife became the distracted mother and did not hesitate to approach the Customs man waiting to check us in. I thought 'is this my wife'? I hardly recognised her. Fur coat flung open, a couple of extra buttons undone at her cleavage and skirts up as she bent down to exclaim 'Oh! My poor darling just look at the state you're in'. 'Please Mr Customs man do you have an unwanted newspaper for her box?' Then to me 'go and buy a toilet roll to clean her up.' Then to the Customs again 'do you have please, please, a saucer of milk for her?' All the time this was going on Cat-Cat was joining in and a little crowd was gathering with the cat lovers leaning over one another's shoulders to see, diverting the Customs Men even more.

Cat-Cat soon realised she was the centre of attention. She was magnificent, despite her inborn suspicion of humans. People seemed to be darting about all over the place on missions on behalf of Cat-Cat including Customs men who, quite obviously were anxious to restore the situation to normality.

Eventually things settled down and the place returned to normal with periodic short meows from Cat-Cat.

Without bothering to offer our bags for examination to the Customs man my wife was effusive with thanks, picked up our things and Cat-Cat and we walked off to find a taxi.

Turning to me my wife said, 'wasn't she a little Darling the way she played up?' then 'I think we were awfully lucky to get through with all that booze and those cigarettes.' It was only then that the penny dropped.

I realised that the normally hardly perceptible lisp which was part of her speaking charm had, during her performance, become most pronounced and her brand new non-duty fur coat had dropped open in a most revealing way quite deliberately. 'Oh, well!'

Much travelled Cat-Cat did not enjoy her short stay with my mother-in-law, being shooed from one resting place to another. Cat-Cat knew only too well she was there on sufferance and was almost calculatedly naughty in her behaviour at the same time ignoring the undisguised hostility of my wife's mum.

We were all rather relieved when it was time to take over our new pub just outside Bath.

Cat-Cat settled down with unmistakable delight in her new surroundings. We had two acres of grounds which had been free of cats for years, the previous owners being dog lovers.

Cat-Cat had established long ago that rats were a push over. She would be gone for hours bringing back her lush harvest of mice at regular intervals and dropping them at the feet of the generously bosomed lady who helped out in the kitchen. She … Cat-Cat … must have known that this very pleasant lady didn't much like cats, and enjoyed the reaction.

As in Guernsey she shunned the bars and the people but condescended to make friends with the staff, her favourite, Antonio, being a young Spanish waiter who spoke softly and cooed to her in Spanish. My wife declared she was trilingual speaking French, Spanish and English.

The relationship between Cat-Cat and Antonio caused some friction between he and Tony our head barman who was also wooing Cat-Cat. Perhaps it was because they both had the same names that she favoured both of them.

Our customers usually met Cat-Cat somewhere around the car park or in the gardens and despite her unapproachability she became quite a feature of the pub. Customers frequently asked after her as if she were just another member of the staff if they had not seen her for some days.

She had by now become a really beautiful cat still remaining slim and elegant but losing some of that kittenish behaviour which her dignified manner could never hide when we first met her.

Then one day she was gone longer than usual. Cat-Cat did not appear. Customer's enquiries fostered our anxieties and after more than 24 hours we began to really worry.

Tony, our head barman, was more distracted than anyone and the next we knew he had organised a mass search of the surrounding district for the coming Sunday morning with all our male customers taking part.

It was a sort of 'drag' but after many hours this search drew a blank. That evening, in the bar, talk was of nothing else and there were many sombre faces bent over pint pots around the bar.

Cat-Cat did not return home.

An air of gloom pervaded the pub both amongst the staff and the customers. Some people we had never seen before came to ask news of Cat-Cat.

It was weeks later we were given a clue as to what had happened to Cat-Cat. It seems someone had seen a dead black cat being thrown into a dust-cart on a lane some distance away from us and the other side of the railway line which ran along the boundary of our pub.

Enquiries to the dustmen seemed to confirm that it *was* Cat-Cat. That side of the railway line was unfamiliar territory to her and we supposed she had been caught unawares crossing the road.

We were very sad.

It was not long after the loss of Cat-Cat that we were told of my wife's terminal illness. This meant leaving the pub and it was some time after that, and after her death that I was again to enjoy the company of cats in the home.

For a period I adopted what might be described as a 'nomadic' way of life. I lived in digs, stayed with friends, and was because of that, unable to have a cat of my own to talk to and share my troubles and my sadness.

I remember when staying in one place, I used after dinner to go for an evening walk. One evening I met 'Ginge'. Ginge was sitting on a low wall surveying his territory (for he was obviously a tom). I approached him slowly talking quietly, and with an extend hand. As I walked towards him he rose from his sitting position and slowly walked towards me, tail erect and head on one side. His body language said 'I wonder if he's OK?'

We stood and faced one another and soon I was gently stroking his head between his ears. This is not my usual approach to a strange cat because a gesture towards the head for many animals is interpreted as an aggressive act. Cats will shy away and some dogs will snap. But this one was different for as we approached one another he had raised himself off his front legs to meet me rubbing his face against my outstretched hand.

He seemed to want companionship as much as I did.

The following night I again took the same route to my walk and low and behold there was Ginge sitting, as I had met him the previous night, on his low wall. Once more we followed the same procedure. I stayed longer that evening talking to him. Before long my evening meeting with Ginge became an essential part of my day and he never failed to be there waiting for me. Eventually he allowed me to sit on the wall beside him. Some of the neighbours had noticed my evening tête-à-tête and, when passing, smiled benevolently but had been considerate enough not to interrupt us.

Chapter Six

FRITZ AND FI-FI IN FARNHAM, SURREY

When I first met my next wife-to-be she had a kitten on her shoulder. It was a little round bundle of black fur with yellow eyes. As I advanced to stroke the squeaking bundle I almost fell over an equally small black and white bundle at her feet. I bent down picked it up and immediately it relaxed putting its tiny front legs either side of my neck.

Future wife said 'I'm glad you like her *this* one is my favourite,' and then she told me the story of how she had acquired. 'Fritz' and 'Fi-Fi'.

She had, she said, been told that a number of kittens were wanting homes at a farm just outside the town. As she had decided she wanted two cats to ease her loneliness she had gone along, chosen two black males and said 'I'll collect them tomorrow.' On returning the following day one of the black ones had already been sold and she had no alternative but to accept.what was left … and that was Fi-Fi.

Fi-Fi's coat was slightly longer and less dense than Fritz's so didn't look so smart. Fritz's coat was.shiny, short, dense and he knew he came from a better litter than Fi-Fi. To make matters worse future wife encouraged him.

In future wife's eyes Fi-Fi was a second class citizen. Fi-Fi was accident prone, she was also clumsy, loose limbed, agile adventurous and loved hunting.

In the years that followed whenever she misbehaved or got into trouble or failed to be the kind of cat which my wife would have liked her to be she was accused of being 'inbred' and 'being from a bad litter' and 'not a thoroughbred like your step brother Fritz'.

Fritz didn't immediately take to me and remained aloof for some time. Eventually he accepted me as being part of the family, and probably a necessity, but it must have been some six years before he began to melt towards me But that is another tale for later on.

In the meantime, of course, as you might well imagine without me having to mention it, I befriended Fi-Fi. I always stood up for her and tried to see that she got equally fair treatment with Fritz.

It is almost a reflex action of mine to favour the undercat. I take no pride nor deserve praise for this attitude ... I just can't help it. I suppose, to a lesser degree I'm that way towards humans.

Fritz continued to remain aloof except to my wife and made it clear he was unconcerned about the adulation of adult humans whilst Fi-Fi fell about with anxiety to be noticed and to be fondled and didn't care who did it.

I've found many humans fall into one of these categories.

Throughout the rest of her life Fi-Fi's pattern of behaviour was to remain unchanged. There was little doubt that from the moment I rescued her from the floor when we first met, and proved, so far as I was concerned, she was loved equally as much as Fritz, I was to be her chosen one and her 'mentor'.

Even before we were married, my wife and I argued about the unfairness of Fi-Fi having to wait for her meal until Fritz had finished his. I said it was reminiscent of that situation in a family where no one was allowed to eat until 'your father' had had his which he expected to be waiting for him on the table when he walked through the door after leaving work.

This attitude of mine was only the beginning of a series of events which further added to the reason why Fi-Fi always came to me. There was never any question of on whose lap which of the cats would decide to sit.

Eventually my little house in Farnham in Surrey was ready for occupation and my wife and I moved in. The upstairs/downstairs situation with Fritz and Fi-Fi continued.

It was now we were to experience the first of many major mishaps to Fi-Fi.

We had been out for the day. There had been a carnival in the town and many motor-bikes and a lot of noise.

We had not worried unduly about the kittens who were by then nearly two for we had fitted a cat flap to the rear door so they had freedom to come and go.

Perhaps I should pause here to describe how our little house was situated. It was in a quiet road semi-detached and had a small garden at the rear, with a rickety gate opening on to Farnham Park ... some 185 acres of it. There was no possibility of preventing the cats from wandering into the Park if they wished. A public footpath in the park ran along the other side of our low wall. To our friends we used to joke that our garden was of 185 acres.

But I've digressed. Normally when we returned Fi-Fi, if she was around, would scamper out to greet us but not on this occasion. We were not worried because we assumed she was out in the garden. Fritz we found asleep in his box and it was some considerable time before we again mentioned Fi-Fi's absence.

She had not come to calls for her in the garden, then, for no particular reason, I went into the guest room. There she was, covered in blood, moaning and unable to move from her place on a bed. Her leg hung down in an awkward position. She had evidently been hit by a car or a motor-bike and had dragged herself home through the cat flap and up the stairs. A considerable feat with a dislocated or broken leg.

Off we rushed to the Vet expecting to hear the dreaded news that she would have to be 'put down'. No such thing, for after an anxious wait for an assessment of an X-Ray the Vet emerged to say 'if you are prepared to nurse her properly for some time whilst her leg mends then she can live'.

As it happened I was then in the early stages of what was going to be a long convalescence following an operation. What better? Fi-Fi and I could recover together. But Fi-Fi was going to be a much more troublesome patient than I.

Fortunately the weather was good so I made her a cage of chicken wire. At first the sides were too high and she tried despite her splint to climb up the wire. So I lowered the height of the sides, put on a top and this allowed her to stand up but not climb.

Through all this anxious period Fritz remained indifferent, in fact there was very little reason why he should have been otherwise for he still received favours from my wife. The only sign we had from him that there was anything different was his interest in the cage.

On his visits to Fi-Fi he would slowly and daintily step around the cage taking periodic sniffs at the wire. Once or twice he stood on his hind legs as if to determine whether or not he could gain access from the top. Having completed his inspection he would settle down with his back to the cage and *that* so far as *he* was concerned was the end of it.

He seemed to know that this, so far as Fi-Fi was concerned was the most irritating thing he could do, for Fi-Fi, poor thing, was constantly struggling to get out and Fritz's freedom, so ostentatiously flaunted in front of her must have been a constant reminder of her position.

But, despite this, I do not believe there was any feeling of resentment or malice towards Fritz. Fi-Fi's character was too simple to rise to that. One of the alternative names given to her by my wife was 'pea brain' and 'flea bag', the latter not because she *was* a flea bag but because, with her loose slightly long hair she was a *potential* flea bag. We gave her constant attention and eventually decided to give her a flea collar to wear … and there too hangs another story.

After many weeks of careful nursing Fi-Fi, except for a permanent twist to her walk which I thought was rather sexy, was back to normal. They were then two years old and growing quite big, much too big, as my wife frequently reminded me, for Fi-Fi to be behaving like a crazy siamese kitten by climbing up the curtains.

The second of the three incidents which marked our stay at the house in Farnham concerned Fritz.

I must explain here that so far as Fritz was concerned my wife had no will power. She would declare Fritz must *not* do this or that, or Fritz *must* do this or that, but in the end. Fritz did just as he wished, and my wife hadn't the will to stop it. He always got his own way and it was on just such an occasion that we lost Fritz.

The weather was awful. It was very cold. It was pouring with rain. It seemed to have been pouring with rain for ever. The tortoiseshell ferral which had been roaming the park and terrorising every domestic cat in the neighbourhood had not been seen for days. Everyone hoped he had died of exposure.

Fritz had developed a chest complaint and the Vet's instructions were 'coddle him he'll get better'. Fritz hated being confined and fretted and complained about being kept in for we had locked the cat flap. Fritz fussed and scratched at the cat flap. He refused, until he nearly burst, to use the dirt tray my wife had so lovingly prepared for him, and when he did I could swear he deliberately made a mistake which of course he didn't cover by scratching.

Fritz didn't let up, so of course eventually my wife succumbed and despite the cold, the rain and the wind … let him out. Almost immediately he vanished. Nor did he return, as my wife.was convinced he would, once having met his natural needs.

As I remarked earlier, at the bottom of our garden with only a very insecure and ineffective fencing between us was the 185 acres of Farnham Park. Wearing a raincoat with a hood and wellingtons my wife stood calling him, trying to fit her calls in between the gusts of wind which drowned her dulcet tones.

My wife asked me to join in the calling but as I had strongly opposed the idea of letting him out I did not see why I should be involved.

By this time my wife was frantic, dashing into the gardens up and down the road on both sides with no result. Seeing how distracted she was I forgot my pride and joined in the search.

Soon both of us were drenched and I had covered most of the ground already covered by my wife. We had been into the Park too and all to no avail. An hour or two must have passed and by this time my wife, most unusually was in floods of tears blaming herself for letting him go.

As we stood outside the backdoor wondering where else to look we heard the faintest of sounds, hardly perceptible and certainly not recognisable as a meow. We lifted a small upturned footbath and there he was, warm and dry with an expression on his face as much as to say 'what's all the fuss about?'

Yet another cat crisis was over.

I seem not to have described Fritz and Fi-Fi in much detail. Fritz of course is easy. He was growing, partly, I kept repeating, into a big cat because of overfeeding. He was pure black except for half a dozen white hairs on his chest which my wife was convinced saved him from the witches. He had a shiny black dense coat. His eyes were yellow and his nose black and he had a rather 'prissy' way of walking due, I used to argue, to him being overweight. (Have you noticed how some fat men have the same prissy walk?) Nevertheless he was almost always dignified in his manner. Fi-Fi's markings were attractive and orderly. Her chest and front legs were pure white and there was a collar of white around her neck. The black markings on her head were rather like a cap which had slipped over one eye. Her back was covered by a black coat and she had a long black tail. She also had the most delightful little pink nose which was accentuated by a habit she had of allowing the tip of her pink tongue to show from time to time. She was a cat well marked, and undeserving of the contempt with which my wife repeatedly treated her.

Life in Farnham was pleasant for the cats and for us but after a time we noticed how jumpy both the cats were becoming looking apprehensively in the direction of the cat flap at the slightest sound

Once or twice.we had.noticed a tomcat smell and the sound of night time encounters were frequent, and from time to time loud enough to awaken us. As my wife on one occasion remarked during a particularly prolonged encounter 'You know … Rossini when he wrote his Péchés de ma vieillesse must have been a cat lover and suffered like us so he included his Cat's Duet'.

But, when Fritz came hurtling through the cat flap one evening skidding across the kitchen floor and rushing up the stairs we knew something was wrong and the situation had become serious. Fritz was not a frightened cat.

I rushed to the window just in time to catch a glimpse of the biggest cat I had ever seen in my life leaping over the fence into the park.

Consultations with our neighbours confirmed our suspicions … a wild cat was on the rampage. It seemed that many people whose houses backed on to the park and who had a cat were worried so we organised a 'Neighbour Cat Watch'. We all agreed to keep a constant lookout for the monster and to phone one another when he was seen.

No one admitted ownership of 'The Terror' or 'The Monster' as we called him and everyone wanted to see him gone for he was causing mayhem amongst the cat population. Cats were returning home bitten and scratched and an epidemic was developing of what could only be described as 'Catagoraphobia'.

I had put food in the shed and one day I managed to corner him there. It wasn't he who was frightened but me as he fixed me with those yellow eyes and seemed to be preparing to pounce.

He was a dirty ginger with a few white stripes, big paws and stood two or three inches taller than most cats. He had a huge head and a fluffy tail. His ears were torn to shreds and his big black nose was out of keeping with the rest of his looks.

His unkempt appearance and rangy look left no doubt in my mind he was a wildcat living rough. He smelt. Perhaps, I thought swiftly, he was one of a litter born rough from what had been a domesticated cat one or two generations back. Here was undoubtedly a survivor.

I was so fascinated I let him go and oddly, I felt sorry for him.

When I reported the meeting to our neighbours they wanted him killed. I could see the unspoken criticism in their eyes. Why hadn't I dealt with him there and then?

They said, as I had seen him and had been largely responsible for organising the Neighbourhood Cat Watch and seemed to have become the leader in the campaign the duty of calling in the R.S.P.C.A. naturally fell upon me. I found it difficult to argue, thinking to myself 'if they knew all about this long before me and had done nothing then if I refuse, nothing will be done'. So I called the R.S.P.C.A.

I suggested they might shoot him with a tranquiliser gun and then put him down. The R.S.P.C.A. said 'catch him and we'll look at him and then decide whether to put him down or rehabilitate him'. Fine! But who was to catch him?

A cat-owners' meeting was held and in the end it fell to me to do something. We decided to catch him if we could.

After a while I could see what I had to do.

I must first explain that our house was very small.

The kitchen was at the back of the house looking on to a narrow garden which backed on to the 185 acres of Farnham Park, as I have already explained.

An extension had been built on to the kitchen which included first a bath room, then a lavatory and on to the wall of the lavatory had been built a lean-to shed.

I had fitted three cat flaps. One between kitchen and bathroom one between bathroom and lavatory and one between lavatory and shed and in the shed I had cut an aperture large enough for the cats to gain access to the first cat flap from the garden.

On more than one occasion my wife and I had noticed a strong smell of 'tom' in the bathroom and as Fritz was a very clean cat it was obvious 'The Monster' had discovered the 'access' procedure.

What I had to do was trap 'The Monster' in the bathroom on one of his nightly visits to Fi-Fi who was now his current attraction. His usual time for visiting was around two in the morning.

First I had to fix a flap over and above the cat flap between the bathroom and the lavatory which would permit entry but which could be dropped to prevent exit thus, keeping him in the bathroom. I fixed a little bell to the cat flap which could be heard in the kitchen.

I then fixed solid the cat flap in the door between kitchen and bathroom so that when the kitchen/bathroom door was closed 'The Monster' would be trapped in the bathroom. This plan was based on the assumption that anyone waiting in the kitchen heard the bell on the bathroom/lavatory cat flap and was so able to quickly close the kitchen door.

The door to the rest of the house from the kitchen would be closed so that if 'The Monster' did gain access to the kitchen he could be driven back to the bathroom.

To the top of the door between bathroom and kitchen I fixed a string long enough to reach the kitchen table on which I had placed a reclining chair. Fixing the string was tricky as the door closed towards the bathroom so it had to run around a nail in the door jamb.

My intention was to sit in the chair, in the dark, wait for the bell to ring, watch for the cat's shadow as it entered the kitchen and then make a noise which I hoped would frighten the cat back into the bathroom. I would then close the door with the string thus trapping the Monster in the bathroom.

I had already filled the bath with cold water.

Once having trapped 'The Monster' in the bathroom with the door closed I would have time to don my protective clothing of leather gloves bowler hat and face mask.

Entering the bathroom I would catch the cat and throw it in the bath. The theory was that the cat would be so preoccupied with trying to swim I would have time to wrap it around with a thick blanket sufficiently to keep it safe until the R.S.P.C.A. arrived next day.

I had even remembered that all the toiletries on the shelves must be removed in case the cat jumped on them in the chase.

I had however overlooked the problem arising when either of us wished to use the lavatory so I provided my wife with a 'pottie' just in case.

What actually happened of course was very different.

The mechanics worked perfectly and I practised getting on and off the table.

At midnight I said good night to my wife who was convulsed with laughter at the thought of me sitting in the chair on top of the table in brown gloves, bowler hat and face mask. I had to explain I wasn't going to do that.

As she went up to bed I asked her to close the kitchen door behind her to prevent 'The Monster' getting into the rest of the house. I said 'are the cats in?' and she replied 'Yes darling and good hunting and good night'.

Sitting in the dark was boring and I became sleepy. I have forgotten to mention that at the last minute in order not to lose the string from the door completely should I get sleepy and drop it, I had given it a loop around my slipper. In fact I then realised I could close the door by bringing up my knee.

I had plenty to think about and it seemed only a short time before the cat flap bell rang I was alert. I was tense. I silently eased myself up and watched for the expected shadow to appear. It did. In the dark it seemed smaller. I allowed it to walk past me I held my breath.

In my excitement I pulled on the string forgetting the cat should be in the bathroom and not in the kitchen. I had also forgotten the loop around my slipper. The tug I gave the string pulled my leg sideways to such a position I found difficulty in getting down and releasing the string. I nearly fell off the table and in the. process knocked the torch, which I intended to use, on to the floor losing it in the dark.

The door closed with a bang as I lost one of my slippers. The cat was cowering against the door leading to the house. I advanced cautiously towards it. Only then did I realise it was Fritz. Fritz seemed as surprised as me and not prepared to be friendly. I opened the door and let him into the house.

Quite obviously my elaborate idea was not going to work. My wife had been wakened by the noise and coming down and being told what had happened said 'all you have to do is sit on the table wait for him to come in get down and he'll run back into the bathroom'. having delivered that pearl of wisdom she went back to bed to comfort Fritz.

I got on to the table. After an hour I began to get sleepy. I probably dozed off and at 4 o'clock I decided to give up and went to bed, concluding that my 'farce with Fritz' had frightened him off.

In the kitchen in the morning there was a dreadful smell of tom cat and the food which I had given Fritz before letting him into the house and forgotten, was all gone. There were also dirty paw marks all around the bath surround and I imagined he had helped himself to a drink to show his contempt.

Shortly after that and for no particular reason 'The Monster' stopped calling but he was seen wandering the neighbourhood. I do believe he realised we were after him and he reckoned caution was the better part of valour.

I still think sadly about the poor old cat.

Undoubtedly he was a thumping nuisance and the constant pressure all of us put upon him must have made his life not worth living so he moved away to easier pastures.

I had admired his audacity and his courage and his ability to survive but I could imagine him getting old and tired and unable to fight for his place in the universe, being less able to defend himself and eventually dying in the corner of some derelict warehouse unloved, unwanted, and unmourned.

I suppose I felt more particularly sensitive about these imaginings setting them alongside the love and care which was bestowed upon Fritz and Fi-Fi. Why did 'The Monster' have to live and suffer in this way? He couldn't have been happy.

It is said recalcitrant children are the product of tough and unloving backgrounds. Did 'The Monster' epitomise the argument?

And, also, each of us has his or her own dark shadow of imagined fear, about which we tell no one. In my case I saw reflected in the fate of 'The Monster' my own dark shadow.

Chapter Seven

FRITZ AND FI-FI IN THE PUB

I don't know what decided us to buy a pub but we did. It was in South Devon. Like the house we were leaving it was small with extremely limited living accommodation but with lots of barns and two acres of land on which was a touring caravan site.

By this time Fritz and Fi-Fi had become sizeable young cats. They adopted their new home immediately and began establishing their territories. Fi-Fi particularly loved the two acres of caravan site which was bounded on one side by a stream. Either side of us there was a farm with many barns and these, of course, were a wonderful source of fun, excitement and mice. She played all day long, wandering from the site into the surrounding fields and orchards.

Fritz seemed to be getting lazier and lazier, making token raids on birds, squirrels, rabbits and whatever didn't move too fast for he was getting fat.

The first problem we encountered was once again how to provide access and ingress for the cats. Security forbade us having a catflap in any of the ground level doors or windows

Eventually the answer presented itself and to our surprise proved a regular source of entertainment to the families who used our covered beer garden at the rear of the pub.

Our bedroom in the flat above was at the back and the window overlooked the flat roof of the kitchen extension below. The kitchen adjoined a barn the upper part of which was used as an office and was reached by exterior wooden steps.

Access for Fritz and Fi-Fi into the house was up the steps, on to a plank which ran around the outside of the barn ('a cat walk!' as some enlightened person proclaimed) to a sloping plank leading down to the flat roof.

The cats then crossed the roof to another sloping plank which led up to a platform outside the bedroom window. In the bedroom window was a catflap.

Early teaching efforts were hilarious. We started putting them through the catflap from inside the bedroom window. Fritz couldn't see the point and kept coming back through the catflap and Fi-Fi sat imperiously on the platform surveying the scenery and refusing to come back through the catflap or go beyond the platform.

After a number of abortive efforts I was left no alternative but to get on to the flat roof, stand outside the window and as my wife pushed the cats through the flap, escort the cats, one my one, across the roof up the plank and around the cat walk.

By this time a laughing staff had gathered to watch my antics supporting me with cries of encouragement as I tiptoed across the flimsy roof from one end to the other pulling and pushing the protesting cats.

Each time we repeated the operation to get them used to the idea a cheer was raised as a cat appeared through the flap. Needless to say the noise served to confuse the cats and the people below only added to their reluctance to take part.

My position on my hands and knee at one moment did not do my dignity with the staff and the cats any good at all. The cats thought I was giving a very poor imitation of their own feline agility and the staff were undoubtedly delighted to see me on my knees, cut down to size.

As I remarked, the catflap gave access to our bedroom. Our bedroom was very small and my bed was close to the window with the foot of the bed near to the catflap.

It was not long before I began to regret the idea for once the cats, particularly Fi-Fi, had become accustomed to using the flap they were in and out during the night jumping on to the end of my bed and, more often than not, on to my feet

I was constantly being woken up.

I remember, on one occasion, being wakened by a screaming wife calling 'get them off of me, get them off ' to find that a full scale cat fight was in progress with three cats (only one of which was ours) sorting out their differences on her bed.

Despite the complexity of exit and entry into the house via the cat walk system it was not unusual for Fi-Fi to bring live animals into the house such as birds, mice, rats and, rabbits and to take them to the bathroom where she released them in the bath, sometimes chasing the terrified animals round and round until she got bored.

It then fell upon us to remove the animals either alive or dead. It reminded me of the 'wall of death' motor cycle entertainment of years ago.

Either it was beneath Fritz's dignity or beyond his ability to catch his own mice but he was always prepared to watch Fi-Fi sitting on the lavatory seat with a superior expression on his face and then, when she had left, to have his own fun with the poor little animal but in a more restrained, half bored … 'this is really beneath my dignity' manner.

It was one of these bathroom visits by Fritz which got him into more trouble than he bargained for.

My wife had gone to have a bath, found a mouse there, removed it, run the bath and got in. She had left the bathroom door open … Fritz had come in and without pausing, jumped on to the bath edge, expecting to retrieve his mouse, slipped on the wet side and finished up by using my wife as a convenient raft to stop drowning.

Fritz had to be rescued, dried off secretly and allowed to occupy the office without Fi-Fi knowing, until such time he had recovered his dignity. All the assurances by my wife to Fritz that a really lovely book had been written about an Otter failed to pacify him.

As I have described, the kitchens were at the back of the pub and a full run of windows overlooked the beer garden. They were in full view of the public so an unwavering high standard of hygiene had to be maintained. Animals were strictly forbidden anywhere near … even Fritz and Fi-Fi.

Anyway, on this day they *did* get in … someone had left the door open. I remember my horror, as on walking through the beer garden putting on my best smile and most regal manner (like the Queen giving a little wave of her hand to her subjects) to the customers gathered there, I saw Fritz and Fi-Fi on the kitchen work-top in full view at either end of a fillet steak which had been removed from the refrigerator for preparation for lunch.

I've never yet worked out why I had to take the blame for this but I did, I recollect being told that as *I* was to blame I must do without my steak on that day to 'make up'. What a penance!

In the four years we were at the pub a few other incidents stay vividly in my memory.

Without pretending to be macho about this I have always argued that since the time of Adam in Eden it has been the female who encouraged the male into increasingly daring and adventurous activities.

It was like this with Fritz and Fi-Fi.

It could not have been an age difference for they were both the same age. Nor could it have been a health difference for they were both fit and, in fact, it was usually Fi-Fi who was hurt from time to time. If my wife's assessment of their breeding origins was correct then one could only say that Fi-Fi was 'street wise' and Fritz not.

It was always Fi-Fi who was the first to go furthest into the hinterland around our property. It was Fi-Fi who found the hollow dead tree on the caravan site and enticed Fritz in, and because he was fatter than her, couldn't get out without being pulled out.

It was Fi-Fi who enticed Fritz on to the caravan site, and it was Fritz who pretended he was a Big Hunter and did a lot of hiding behind bushes and clumps of grass wriggling his fat bottom and convincing no one but himself he was about to catch the bird which was temptingly feeding a few feet away from him.

I remember my wife's look of horror as, discoursing as I was prone to do from behind the bar to amuse my customers, I was relating Fritz's antics and how he waited for Fi-Fi to provide his 'sport'. Warming to my subject I said it reminded me of one of those landowners who breed pheasants on their estate and had beaters to find the birds and drive them towards him whilst he was sitting with his fat bottom on his shooting stick.

I was reminded later that some of the customers in our pub were just what I had been describing. 'Did I really want the business?' I was asked. And 'why not stick to animal stories?' I was told.

Truth is always stranger than fiction and funnier too if you have the right sense of humour. Unfortunately that moment of slap-stick humour which at the time has us rolling about and splitting our sides is always difficult to describe in words. Just such a one happened to Fritz. As I have remarked, Fritz had begun to use the gardens regularly and one day on arriving on the lawn he came face to face with a squirrel.

Animals as everyone knows, when in danger, do not do what one would expect of them to avoid or escape … take a rabbit in the car's headlights for example

I had been sitting on the lawn with Fritz not far away when the squirrel arrived. I kept very still. Fritz and the squirrel seemed equally surprised at finding themselves within a short distance of one another and in the open.

At first the squirrel stood on its back legs front paws drawn up in the familiar stance and stared at Fritz. It remained there quite motionless for what seemed a long time, and stared at Fritz.

Fritz stared back. He had never, to my knowledge, seen a squirrel before. This was not a bird. It was not a mouse. Time for both of them, stood still whilst they absorbed the situation, summing one another up rather like two boxers in the ring before the bout commences

Not a whisker of Fritz quivered. Not a twitch to the squirrel's tail. I froze. Then the squirrel's nose and whiskers began working overtime. For a moment both squirrel and Fritz had forgotten my presence. Slowly, very very slowly, Fritz raised his bottom to a pouncing position his tail twitching at the tip close to the ground. Then the tail became rigid and the movement was transferred to his bottom which began the familiar wriggle from side to side.

The squirrel still hadn't moved and stayed there as if mesmerised whilst Fritz moved first one paw and then the other almost imperceptibly forward keeping his gaze firmly on the squirrel.

Two more stealthy slow motion movements followed before the squirrel decided 'enough was enough' and darted towards and to the left of Fritz. This move confused Fritz who had expected, no doubt, from his past experiences, that his prey would run away and not towards him. But this was too late for, at the very second that the squirrel had moved forward, Fritz had begun his pounce towards where the squirrel should have been. Fritz pulled up short to find the squirrel running in a curve behind him. Fritz started to follow the squirrel in its circular route.

At least two circuits were performed by both animals, Fritz, a few feet behind the squirrel, before the squirrel spotted his escape route … a tree. But a wider circuit had to be performed, before the squirrel was ready for the run up the tree, and by now Fritz had gathered speed.

Unfortunately for big Fritz he wasn't as agile as the squirrel which darted up the tree. Fritz was close behind but his momentum was too great to take avoiding action before he ran head on into the tree almost knocking himself out. I'm sure the squirrel was up there laughing himself silly. It was Disney Cartoon stuff and I regretted not having a cine-camera handy.

Once again poor Fritz's dignity had been shaken and not improved by my calling him a 'silly old fool' when he crossed the lawn to me for sympathy.

Dogs were not permitted in the pub and only on leads in the beer garden and on the caravan site, so the cats didn't run much risk when they used the cat walk, but,there was one occasion when things *did* go wrong that bears recounting.

Some good customers of ours had come to stay and they had a dog. A big black retriever whose favourite lunch would have been a cat if only he could have caught one. His persistence and enthusiasm in chasing them without success could only be admired.

Naturally Big Black Dog was kept on a lead but on this occasion the parents gave the lead to their young daughter issuing strict instructions 'not to let it go or move from where you are sitting'. This was sensible for there were other dogs in the beer garden.

Naturally, and needless to say, as so often happens when things go wrong, it was a combination of unusual circumstances which led to the uproar which ensued.

The daughter decided to put the lead loop under a chair leg whilst she went to buy a soft drink. The chair was a light plastic one. Whilst she was gone both Fritz and Fi-Fi came down the steps from the office. They had barely reached the bottom before Big Black Dog spotted them. With a joyful yelp he dived for the cats dragging the chair which upset the table, which upset more chairs and smashed some glasses. The sudden noise and barking immediately excited the other dogs one of which, held too lightly by another customer, got free and tore through the legs of other customers dragging with it the long lead which began to tangle with customers' legs.

One customer who had. attempted to rise, was half risen when his chair tipped over. People stood up. Dogs barked. Cats and dogs seemed, to be going in every direction and the man holding a third dog found the lead wound around his legs.

Beer, glasses, tables and chairs were going everywhere and everyone was shouting advice and making ineffective attempts to restrain the animals.

Someone had left open the door at the side of the pub and the passage led to the road. Both cats spotted the escape route and took it pursued by the two dogs. Fortunately as they fled across the road there was no traffic. The cats flew to the top of the wall and vanished in the garden. The dogs stood below barking their frustration and gradually things calmed down.

As my wife remarked later, referring to the garden into which the cats had fled 'they *would* go in there, you *know* Peter *hates* cats!' as if the whole event was my fault.

This little event nearly lost us our Black Dog customers for it was with the greatest effort I managed to restrain my wife from ordering them to leave and never to return. All that my wife could think about was that her Fritz had been frightened, nearly eaten by a dog and might have been run over.

One of the pleasant things about running a pub is the occasional gift brought by one's customers. Being in the country it was not unusual for a farmer friend to bring us a brace of pheasants.

By mid October we were less busy so the pheasants were hung in the beer garden. No sooner were they there than Fritz settled down beneath them. I'm sure he enjoyed the smell and made the most of the occasional drip but he never attempted to get one down. No doubt he thought it was a good place to be 'just in case one of them fell'.

Nearby to where the pheasants were hung there was a 5 ft stone wall, dividing us from the farm next door. In the evenings during the season Fi-Fi would lie on the wall waiting for a low flying house marten. She was incredibly agile and one of her tricks was to leap from the wall in the hope of catching a bird in flight. At least that was the theory but she rarely succeeded in doing so. As someone who had been a witness to the Big Black Dog event, Fi-Fi's optimism matched that of Big Black Dog.

The sight of Fi-Fi in flight reminded me of the Opossum as it flies from tree to tree. When I commented on this to my wife she said simply to have such fanciful ideas was proof of how besotted I was with the cats.

Fi-Fi's adventuring spirit finally got her into real trouble. Once again coincidence meant that I was the one to rescue her only to strengthen the ties between us.

I have told how she would wander far and wide and of the farm next door. Wild animals in that part of Devon were fairly common and rabbits a real nuisance so periodically a shoot would be organised. On this occasion Fi-Fi had not been seen for some time but we were not anxious, such an absence was not unusual.

I was the far end of the Caravan Site examining a small brook which marked the boundary when I spotted Fi-Fi. She was lying the other side of the fence, her head covered in blood, moaning,

I picked her up cradling her in my arms and she seemed to snuggle gratefully towards me as I murmured soothing words to her. On examination it seemed almost certain she had been shot in the jaw by a 2.2 rifle slug, mistaken, I'm sure for a rabbit. Once more it was off to the vets. Fortunately the damage was not so great and the vet said it would mend.

But then the difficult period of convalescence began for with her strapped jaw I was obliged to feed her with a fountain pen filler. The poor little thing lost weight but we kept her going with Calf's Foot Jelly (of all things) and anything soft which might melt in her mouth.

The adjacent farm where Fi-Fi spent quite a lot of time hunting little animals was a good source of fleas which found a comfortable home in her long loose coat. In the end we had to equip her with a flea collar. We chose a red one and whilst we thought it made her look even prettier and she was much admired, she hated it.

There were lots of cats in the neighbourhood of the pub and ours managed to avoid too many confrontations despite the fact that the smell of food and Fi-Fi's undoubted femininity (she had of course been spayed) our place was a source of attraction to the farm cats who were largely left to fend for themselves.

Whilst Fi-Fi teased the optimistic Toms at the same time maintaining a safe distance Fritz could not resist a good 'night time' fight. He was big and strong and tough. He was also lazy.

On many occasions during the night when a cat fight was in full swing somewhere within hearing distance Fritz, who had been peacefully asleep on my wife's bed, would start up, growl like a dog, leap across from my wife's bed to mine, crash through the catflap and go tearing along the catwalks to join in the disturbance.

In no time at all there would be a few agonised yelps and then silence.

In due course Fritz would reappear, his manner that of someone who has just completed a good business deal and is rubbing his hands together with satisfaction and achievement.

The more Fi-Fi visited the bar and was petted and admired the more often she returned until she became a nuisance getting between people's legs, tripping them up and causing them to spill their drinks. One observant customer asked me if we had trained her to do this!

As my wife remarked to me one day, in order to emphasise the superiority and breeding of Fritz over Fi-Fi … Fritz *never* does that!'

I must admit Fritz behaved himself very well indeed, and I felt a certain sympathy for him because he was incapable of a 'meow', but, as I have told, this did not detract from his fighting ability. Do some boxers come to mind?

We had been four years in the pub. We had worked hard and we felt we needed a rest so, when someone offered to buy we said 'yes'. We soon found a house in Wiltshire and also bought a Mobile Home Site not too far away.

Chapter Eight

FRITZ AND FI-FI IN WILTSHIRE

Because of the difficulty of moving and believe me the difficulties of moving from a house are child's play compared with moving from a Pub, the cats were taken in advance by my wife to a cattery near where we were going to live. The cattery she reported was 'awful' but the only one which, at that time, could accommodate them. We just hoped their stay would not be a long one.

I had, in all the years I had lived with a cat, never before been obliged to use a cattery. In discussing the situation with friends I was assured that most catteries were good and we just must have been unlucky.

Once we arrived in our new house Fritz suddenly found his voice. The noises he made were not impressive, we had to admit and certainly not in keeping with the rest of his appearance, but at least he was able to communicate.

I suggested that perhaps he had objected to being in the cattery so much his protests had 'found voice'.

Although we were in the country there were houses either side of us, all in fair sized gardens and along the lane. The gardens were large in some cases which our cats enjoyed. It was a horsey, doggie area, drinks parties were common and every one was very proper.

Fritz didn't mind his reduction in territory but Fi-Fi, instead of using the woods at the back of the house insisted on crossing the lane into the fields beyond.

Fi-Fi's fascination with the fields opposite soon got her into trouble. As I have said it was a horsey/doggie area and the hunt was active. I am anti fox hunting and just for fun and to confuse the hounds, when I heard the sound of the hunt in the distance I would go out into the garden and blow my hunting horn. Most times it was, I confess, ineffective.

On this particular occasion I had done just that and with some small success but the result was not what I had expected. I was glad my wife was with me to see the tableau which unfolded before us in the field opposite for no one would have believed it possible.

As we watched from the elevated position of our lawn we could see across the lane into the field opposite, We could hear the yelping of a single hound which gave me satisfaction that I had drawn off at least one, but what followed was beyond the creative imagination of any cartoonist.

First to emerge from the copse on the right was the fox followed by Fi-Fi and not far behind a small deer, then in no particular hurry, and seemingly enjoying the fun and following the procession of animals was the hound.

They streamed in a straight line from right to left of the field one behind the other breaking cover and then vanishing again. We were naturally anxious for Fi-Fi but she turned up in due course, for once unharmed, and with an expression of satisfaction and a demeanour which said 'what's all the fuss about?'

I was surprised at the variety of wildlife which abounded in and around our village and delighted when one night my wife beckoned me to the window to look at three badgers which were scuffling about on the front lawn just below the window.

Bread from a bird table had fallen and they were enjoying the feast. From then on we began putting out food for them and gradually they came to accept the bright lights shining from the lounge windows.

I have recounted this story because Fritz too became a regular 'watcher'. As the badgers gradually became accustomed to us we would sit on an upper lawn, under a tree, out of the light.

On our third vigil we were joined by Fritz who came silently out of the shadows and settled down beside us. From then on it was a 'threesome'. It was, during one of these sessions we first became aware of Ginger, as we first called him.

Ginger quite obviously lacked the good manners of Fritz, who had discretely avoided upsetting the Badgers, but Ginger walked up aggressively and frightened them off. He proved later to be a natural bully.

Who was to know what was in Fritz's mind when he first saw this intruder, for not once during our watching vigils had he made any attempt to go near the Badgers, but we had noticed on some occasions he would leave our side quite soon and move around to a different position equally as far away, keeping in the shadows.

We could see his eyes reflected in the lights shining from the windows. We talked about this to a wildlife expert who reminded us that badgers have very poor sight but a highly developed sense of smell. We wondered if Fritz had been aware of this instinctively and gone to windward whilst we were surely fortunate that the badgers failed to pick up our scent.

It seemed that Fritz who had taken a somewhat back seat in the pub was now to assert his personality. His experiments with meowing seemed to give him confidence. As my wife remarked it really was fortunate that this had happened to him for we were in an area where everyone spoke in loud confident voices even if they had nothing to say.

My wife's tendency to put Fritz first made Fi-Fi's sense of inferiority worse … at least *I* thought so. I'm sure I was more aware of it than Fi-Fi which if one wants to philosophise about the relationship between humans and animals, seems to confirm it is the humans who accentuate eccentric behaviour amongst animals reading all kinds of complicated motivations into the animals from which only humans could suffer.

Animals if left alone will sort themselves out.

As I once remarked if humans would study animals and learn some lessons from them instead of trying to achieve it the other way around, people might benefit.

There … its out. I had promised myself I would keep this book free of personal opinions and not make it controversial but, as you will note later it *does* have some bearing on what I have to tell.

As you have no doubt gathered Fritz was not a gregarious personality, neither with humans nor his own kind. We have all met people like that and no doubt spent hours speculating on just why they were like that.

This tendency of humans to imbue animals with human qualities, with if you will, a 'consciousness' is common, but now in recent years it has become a scientific study by philosopher David Chalmers of the University of California at Santa Cruz.

At a conference in Tucson, Arizona the question of what of our actions and reactions were conscious or subconscious and whether or not some of this could simply be instinct came under deep discussion. And of course animal behaviourism came within the scope of the discussions.

If in due course some convincing conclusions emerge from the studies then animal rights groups might well find there is useful material for their campaigning, and Aunt Mary, sitting in her rocking chair with Tibby on her lap, will rest content and convinced that her pet understands every word she is saying to her.

I'm sure it is the sheer natural simplicity of animals' behaviour which makes them so enchanting. Having said *that* I'm reminded of the naughty behaviour of Fritz which one would have sworn was a carefully calculated insult to our next door neighbour demonstrating his disapproval and dislike of people.

As I've remarked drinks parties were frequent in our village and whenever permitted by the weather, they were held on the lawn. The widow next door had two very well bred cats. They had quickly taken second place to street wise Fritz and Fi-Fi, and allowed them the run of their territory.

Fritz had developed a habit of sleeping on a table in the widow's garden for his morning siesta. His annoyance at being disturbed by the preparations for a garden party were apparent.

So … at the next drinks party given by our neighbour Fritz paid a carefully timed visit. He appeared on the lawn amongst all the guests, was admired and petted and having most unusually for Fritz, submitted with little grace, promptly sat down in full view and did what he had undoubtedly been saving up for the occasion.

His body language as he stalked off without bothering to make the gesture of covering it up as cats normally do, said everything.

This little incident had me rushing around with dustpan and brush trying to remove the offending items whilst my wife was making loud and profuse apologies to everyone within sight.

We might have passed this occasion off as purely incidental if it had not happened a second and third time. After that we shut him in the house during drink parties.

When released after the party was over he would sulk, refuse to eat and vanish for the rest of the day. It was then my turn to say to my wife with some relish 'so much for your well bred cat!!'

I have said that Fritz was a fighter; this is true but on arriving at our

Wiltshire house he had found a formidable opponent. This was Ginger the cat who had first appeared at the night time Badger sessions. Ginger had been established for some time and he considered the whole of the area around the lane was his territory. During the years he had lived there he had staked his claim and no cat had yet arrived to dispute his claims. He had no intention of giving up even the smallest portion of it to any newcomers.

Ginger was Ginger. He was a big, slimly built cat. He was powerful and rangy with a swagger which emulated the cowboys in the early Westerns. He also had a very loud and commanding meow.

Ginger was a beautiful specimen. He was afraid of no one, human or animal, and if one tried to shoo him away he stood his ground, stared at one as if to say 'who the hell do you think you are?' … and 'another peep out of you and I'll have you court martialled!' He belonged to the Brigadier four houses down the lane. I wondered if the Brigadier had trained him.

Ginger had been bullying the two little cats next door for a long time and Jackson the dog on the other side was afraid of him despite the fact that he was twice the size of Ginger. Fritz was brave, tried to stand up to Ginger but was no match for him and Fi-Fi was outright terrified of him.

Then arose the occasion when we wondered if we had made a mistake in giving Fi-Fi a collar to wear. Fritz was asleep on the table in our next door neighbour's garden when we left the house to go to the pub for a drink. We had left Fi-Fi in the house. It was summer and we had left windows open and there was of course the cat flap.

When we returned Fritz was still fast asleep on the table and as we approached the house Ginger emerged through the cat flap. The same thought occurred to my wife and myself at the same instant for we both said … 'Fi-Fi' and dashed for the door.

The sight which greeted us was heart rending.

There had obviously been a fight – fur was everywhere. What had happened during the fight one could only surmise but there was my beautiful Fi-Fi almost choking, her jaw pulled firmly down by her collar which had some- how been dragged into that position during the fight and was now acting as a gag.

I quickly released her and after some sponging down the damage was not so bad as it first appeared.

From then on Fi-Fi was a very frightened lady and unwilling to go out of the house very often. I went on a vigorous campaign of chasing Ginger away from our property but Fi-Fi never really lost her nervous reaction to the sound of the catflap knocking as Fritz or the wind moved it

Perhaps there is a hidden message in this story. After the event I certainly gave more thought to the collars worn by Fi-Fi and subsequent cats in my life.

Too loose and the kind of accident just described is a possibility and, of course, in the case of dogs dangerous should they be on a lead and 'slip the lead'. Too tight and the collar becomes a health hazard and is a discomfort and cruel to the animal. Perhaps a visit to the Vet for his/her advice on the correct size is a good idea.

Fi-Fi's ordeal vividly brought to mind my own experience in the Army in India when we were training for unarmed combat during the Burma campaign. I was pretending to be on guard and a colleague was supposed to creep up behind me holding me powerless by my helmet chinstrap knocking me unconscious and without a sound.

My colleague was too enthusiastic and things went wrong as he grabbed me. The helmet rim came down hard against the back of my neck and the chin strap caught in my throat. It was a very effective demonstration for those watching of how to break someone's neck and choke them at the same time.

As someone pointed out later it was only effective if one's target was wearing a British shaped helmet … the Jap helmet was a different shape and therefore the whole demonstration was pointless unless of course you got fed up with a colleague's company.

Finding Fi-Fi as I did I confess to 'seeing red' and despite my love of all cats had Ginger been within reach I would have killed him. I would of course have regretted doing so afterwards as it would have been completely contrary to my beliefs that if one is to love animals … *all* animals … one must appreciate that their actions are not motivated by the complexities and subtleties of we humans … their needs and actions are simple and basic and an animal lover has to accept this. The gentleman in the Zoo who had his arm severed by a big cat forgave the animal because he appreciated the animal's action was a natural one and probably aggravated by his own actions and carelessness.

Fi-Fi seemed to feel the cold more than Fritz. We could only conclude this was because she had a loose less dense coat. There was an Aga in the kitchen and it took only one attempt by Fi-Fi to walk on the Aga top for her to realise her pads were not made of asbestos.

This first experiment resulted in long periods of recuperative licking of her pads supplemented by us by the application of some soothing balm which she promptly tried to lick off.

At night we bound her feet after an application of the balm but by morning the bandages were off spread all over the house.

Never again did she attempt to walk on the Aga but this did not deter her from sleeping on the work top surface as near to the Aga as she could get with her nose hanging over the edge. How she never came to burn her nose I do not know. Had she done so it would have been a pity because it was such a pretty little pink nose.

It was about this time Fritz began to thaw towards me for, as I have explained he had always remained a little aloof, perhaps deterred by the close relationship between Fi-Fi and me, and also by his affection for my wife.

And of course, it seemed always to fall to me to chastise and reprimand him for his various lapses in good behaviour.

I had converted the smallest bedroom into an office and it was around the time of the attack on Fi-Fi that Fritz began to visit me when I was working in the office. Fi-Fi had been a regular visitor for some time and the arrival of Fritz began to provoke complications. Fi-Fi had usually sat or slept on the window sill content with the knowledge that we were in the same room together but Fritz, once he had made up his mind to visit me, decided the togetherness act was to be 'the real thing' and sat on the desktop disturbing or covering up my papers and, if the desk lamp was lit, warming his nose at the bulb. Fi-Fi, feeling she was losing out on the situation would join him on my desk the resultant confusion putting an effective stop to any aspirations of doing work which I might have.

I had just begun to congratulate myself that I had at last got the Ginger Cat problem under control when my wife began a campaign for us to move somewhere nearer to her daughter and son-in-law.

Chapter Nine

FI-FI AND FRITZ IN SUSSEX

In due course we moved to a pretty village near to Midhurst overlooking the South Downs. The house was smaller than the previous one so I had my office in a big shed in the garden.

As I sat at my desk I had a view through the window to the fields beyond. The shed door was glass and it was no time before I was being visited by both Fi-Fi and Fritz, who resumed their positions on my desk causing the now familiar confusion of my papers.

I was also, of course, able to observe their antics in the garden when they were not with me.

Although there were cats in the village none had established territorial rights where we had the house. A cat-flap was installed in the kitchen door and they both came and left at will. Fi-Fi still reacted to the sound of the cat-flap never having forgotten the incident with Ginger in our previous house, but, in general, I believe both cats were happier in our new home than they had been in Wiltshire.

Our house was at the end of the village and they had a free run of fields both back and front although it was usually only Fi-Fi who ventured across the road into the fields beyond.

One of the odd developments was their obvious preference for the shed to take their cat-naps rather than the house. There was nowhere in the shed really soft or comfortable for them to sleep although I do confess to piling up some old jerseys and pullovers for them.

I'm sure the reader who has had cats will have noted the same behaviour pattern with their own cats but they do seem to develop a set of habits when living in one place, and then, if moved will seem to forget those habits and adopt a whole set of new ones in the new environment.

This had happened with Fritz and Fi-Fi. 'The wall of death' syndrome in the bath never reoccurred after leaving the pub. Fitz's demonstrative objection to 'drink parties' never reappeared after leaving Wiltshire. On the other hand their habit of visiting me in my office and using my desk for their siestas continued from Wiltshire to Sussex.

This is a behaviour pattern which I have never been able to fathom, to which to find a logical answer.

Perhaps, as someone suggested to me, they are like humans, simply reacting to the collective set of circumstances and the opportunities offered at the time. If this is true then surely the sociologist has something to learn here.

I have said there were cats in the village and it was not long before they began to visit our house. Needless to say most of them were Toms and the main point of interest was Fi-Fi. One of them had certainly not been neutered for he had come through the cat-flap whilst we were out, no doubt seeking Fi-Fi and left his smelly card around the feeding bowls having cleaned them out first.

We were glad when he lost interest in Fi-Fi and from then on we simply had to put up with the periodic visits of underfed cats from the poorer end of the village, who came through the cat-flap, woofed up the contents of the feeding bowls and left again without so much as a 'thank you'.

Both cats seemed to be happier in their new home and they seemed to gain particular enjoyment from sleeping in the conservatory at the back of the house, when the weather was too bad to be outside and I was not in the shed. Life for all of us was very peaceful.

Fritz had finally accepted and forgiven me. We were good friends. He loved sitting on my desk curling himself around the back of the typewriter not seeming to mind the repeated knocks he received from the carriage as it moved from side to side. As he became used to the situation he became more interested and adventurous in what he would do to become involved with me.

Finally and by accident of course, he discovered the mystery and fascination of a typewriter keyboard. To begin with he would sit close up at one side of the typewriter and as I typed would put a paw up to catch the key as it rose. It did cross my mind that perhaps he had now associated the keys and the movement of the carriage with the repeated knocks he received from it. Was he trying to stop it?

But this was not enough for Fritz and eventually he learned that if he stood on the keyboard with one front leg he could use the other to play with the keys which he had raised leaving them in a horrible jumble which I had then to untangle.

Both cats were by this time approaching 15 years old and whilst Fi-Fi seemed not to be bothered too much by the weight of her years poor Fritz was. He developed severe arthritis in his back legs and going up stairs was obviously painful as he climbed one step at a time to sleep on my wife's bed. He had shown signs of kidney trouble as far back as Wiltshire but seemed to recover. Now he was obsessed by water. He developed a passion for water. He would paddle in his saucer splashing it all over the place and soon we found him in the mornings standing with both front legs in the bird-bath or in puddles if it had been raining. He sought out receptacles or collections of water in the garden. To add to his miseries he began to go deaf.

He seemed increasingly to want comfort and protection but it was to my wife he went when he wanted a lap. The pattern of their affections had not changed over the years, Fritz went to my wife and Fi-Fi came to me.

Relations between my wife and myself had been deteriorating for some time until finally we agreed it would be better if we separated. I was sad to leave, and my sadness was emphasised by the need to leave the cats at a time when they needed all the care and loving we both could give them.

My wife felt this too and on a return visit to discuss the disposal of the house – for she too was moving away – I found that she had taken them to the vet and had them put down. I try and console myself with the thought that this was the inevitable end to their happy lives anyway and to have kept Fritz alive much longer with his miseries was not a kindness, whilst Fi-Fi for all her independent skittishness would I am sure have pined for Fritz and missed the freedom of our situation so essential to her.

I often wonder why pet owners who profess to love their pets persist in keeping alive their loved ones when they have obviously gone beyond the point of enjoying their lives.

I believe an animal's enjoyment of life is essentially bound up with its state of health and the freedom that represents. A human, even when disabled or unwell, can still extract a degree of enjoyment from life through mental occupations.

How far can one relate the emotional problems of an animal to those of our own human loved ones in such a plight?

And so that was the end of the saga of Fi-Fi and Fritz and the beginning of a new life.

I wondered, much later, if the cats had been the cement which had kept us together for so long and I reflected on how, in those later years, we had come to communicate through those two loving and wonderful little creatures.

Chapter Ten

THE CARAVAN PARK AND THE NEW BEGINNING

For the last eight years of the marriage I had owned a Mobile Home Site in Wiltshire. Dogs were not permitted but cats were so it goes without saying there were a lot of cats. Cats of every description, breed, size and sex swarmed over the place and I loved them all.

One of the interesting observations I made was the difference in the way in which the cats were treated and cared for in what was almost identical circumstances. Watching the way in which the different cats coped with the way in which the different owners treated them was fascinating, and illuminating.

Some were well fed whilst others had barely enough to eat. Some spent their time lazing around in their caravan homes whilst others were left outside all day to fend for themselves, scavenging for food, whilst their master or mistress was out at work.

I think one of the most amusing scenes occurred almost daily at between 5 and 6 o'clock in the evening when the working folk returned home.

The car park was at the far end of the Site and the cars had to drive past the caravans to reach it. It was fascinating to watch the various cats spoiled and neglected, wait to recognise their owner's car and go running to meet it, sometimes there would be as many as six or seven of them trooping up the road.

I used to think how cheerless that site would have been without that company of cats, and wondered how important those little creatures were to their owners in bringing some happiness and relaxation into those small homes. I turned a deaf ear to the protests of the garden lovers at the alleged damage the cats did to their plants.

Trying to convince them that the cats' activities would in time become good manure wasn't very successful. My suggestions for keeping them out of their gardens were treated with derision.

There were a number of black cats in the community and I recollect once being faced by an irate red faced gardener waving a shovel, which made me fear for my life, complaining loudly about the activities of one particular black cat which had dug up his bulbs. He wanted 'justice' he roared, waving the shovel. My reply, which surprised both myself and the gardener, helped to defuse the situation most satisfactorily ... it was simply ... 'which one?'

It was not until I had said it, and watched the effect of my comment, in those fleeting seconds which sometimes seem like hours that I realised what a silly and unanswerable reply it was, for to anyone, not owning a cat, all black cats on the Site must have looked alike.

The gardener too must have realised there was nothing he could do about it unless he could identify or catch the offending animal and face the owner.

The best I could do was to offer to replace the bulbs, an offer ungraciously received accompanied by an accusation that it was my fault because he had seen me feeding some of the cats.

This was of course true, I *had* been trying to seek out the underfed ones and supplement their diet. This activity had given me an opportunity to study the cats and I was surprised, after a time, to find that amongst some fifteen of them there had emerged no bully. A 'boss cat' there was not.

The reader will by now, perhaps, have noted a strange thing ... despite my love of cats, never, throughout my life have I deliberately set out to acquire a cat. Cats have come to me by accident. They have been given to me or already have been part of the people and homes where I have lived, or ... they have walked in and taken up residence.

Chapter Eleven

TIGGER – CINDY AND BARNEY

It was the Caravan Site which brought me face to face with the lady with whom I eventually came to live. She had come to buy a vacant caravan. We had talked. I tried to persuade her not to do so. I felt she would not be happy living in a caravan and finally persuaded her to stay in the lovely old chalk cottage she was then renting.

I was invited home to tea and it was then that I was introduced to the most remarkable cat I have ever met.

As we sat sipping tea, taking a sidelong glance at the cat, whose name I learned was Tigger, who was sitting glaring at me from a safe position on the window sill, I asked the inevitable question 'how did you acquire him?'

The lady's name was Claire and apparently when she had come to live in this lovely, isolated old cottage in a remote village in Wiltshire, surrounded by the most beautiful countryside, being a 'cat' person and knowing she would want company, she had gone to the local R.S.P.C.A. to see what they had available. It was not the first time she had visited the R.S.P.C.A. and found a companion.

This is how she told her story.

'As I walked past the cages I had almost got to the end and hadn't seen one I couldn't resist when I saw Tigger. He was sitting bolt upright with that air of authority which he can assume, looking at me with those large beautiful appealing eyes, demanding attention. I didn't hesitate … I was hardly conscious of saying "Him … I'll have him" … he'd hypnotised me.'

'I'd gone prepared with a wicker basket. The R.S.P.C.A. attendant handed me Tigger out of the cage and as I took him into my arms he bit me. Not hard, but a quite definite nip which I felt sure was merely to establish how the relationship was going to be between us. There was no doubt it was going to be one of equals.'

'I asked the Inspector, as I paid for him, where he had come from. He said "he belonged to an old lady who had died. She had had a lot of cats at the time, Tigger was the last of them." '

'From the beginning Tigger was different. Very different. When I got him home he "emerged" from his carrier with great dignity. He didn't come out slowly or tentatively, he didn't refuse, he didn't leap out. He came out looking around as much as to say "where's the reception party" and "I wonder if this will suit me?" I could only think of a Monarch alighting from a Royal Coach.'

'I opened the carrier in the kitchen where there was one of those leather covered high stools which one uses whilst waiting for the 3 minute egg. Without hesitating Tigger jumped up on the stool and sat there. From that day the stool became Tigger's throne and no one was permitted to use it but him.'

I said to Claire 'why did you call him Tigger?' She said 'well – I would like to have called him "Attab" but its not a good recognisable sound for a cat, he wouldn't have understood. So … I thought he had tiger markings, that's why.' Then with a pause … she said … 'do you know where the word "tabby" originated?' I said 'No! tell me'.

'Apparently,' she said, 'it dates back almost 2000 years to a time when silk was being manufactured in Baghdad and it had a special design and stripe, a colour like a tabby cat. The quarter of Baghdad in which it was made was called "Attābīy" deriving its name from a minor prince named Attab.' 'In case you doubt it,' she said with a giggle, 'he was the son of Omēyyā.'

When I came to check this I found it was all true. (*See official and full explanation in the Catiopedia at the end of the book.*)

And so it came to pass that with Tigger's permission I took up residence in the chalk cottage with his mistress Claire.

At first he was quite obviously both jealous and suspicious of my presence and I realised that living with Tigger would be an experience and a challenge I had never before met.

It was not a question of sharing one's life with a cat. One had the feeling that here was a cat with the power of personality which made one feel there was another human in the home and not 'just a cat'.

He made one feel that if one was going out the matter had first to be discussed with him, and that he deserved an explanation of how long one would be gone and where one was going.

As a visiting friend remarked … 'Its a little scary'.

'Kitchen time' as Claire and I came to call the times he joined us sitting on his stool, seemed one of his greatest delights. He would sit on his haunches on his throne and as one passed close by a paw would flash out complete with claws and one's hand would be drawn gently to his mouth where he would give a little nip, a lick and a nuzzle.

Tigger tolerated his head being stroked, but hated anyone touching his back. Anyone attempting to stroke him would receive a vicious bite or a quick flick from a paw with claws extended. We consulted a vet who whilst not finding anything wrong said there may have been memories of pain in the past or it might be memory of ill treatment in the past by a previous owner.

Tigger's marking was perfect. I had never before seen such symmetry, such delicate golden brown and black shading. His coat shone and the markings which came from around the 'collar' were like a mayoral chain whilst the streaks which came evenly over his head were similar in shape to those on a cobra's hood.

Tigger was one of the most powerful, most muscular cats I have ever had the privilege of meeting. He was unlike the big cats such as tigers and lions who are lithe with powerful shoulder muscles. Tigger was built more like a bulldog. Whilst his body was big, solid and muscular he had slim rather prissy legs and the most delicate of paws.

His eyes were large and whereas most cats eyes are only large when light intensity is at the minimum Tigger's seemed always to be wide open, and this seemed to emphasise the intensity and beauty of their deep amber colouring

He had a habit of looking at one with eyes wide open in a long unbroken stare giving the impression he could understand every word said to him.

The care he took over his appearance was that of a dandy, He was fastidious about his feet which he was frequently treating to the most vigorous pedicures, the chief feature of which was the removal of unwanted nail follicles.

He would sit with paw spread out biting and tugging at a claw and making loud clicking noises as he did so. We never did teach him to carry out this performance in the garden and so Claire was constantly going around the house with a dustpan and brush sweeping up the bits which would be found anywhere from the bedcover in the guest's bedroom to the centre pages of the Radio Times.

Perhaps his most endearing feature was his pale pink nose which was quite out of keeping with the rest of his impressive appearance. It really belonged to a delicately built female. But most of all there was his tail.

Like his legs and his paws and his nose his tail seemed not to belong to him. It was long and stemmed from a powerful base finishing in a delicately pointed tip. What distinguished it was its restlessness. Almost all the time at least an inch or so of it was twitching and moving even when he was asleep.

It was as though Tigger's tail was something with a life of its own. I almost came to believe this. Tigger's tail did all the things which most other cats' tails do but more.

It would lie quiet only occasionally. When seemingly asleep it gave the message 'you may think I'm asleep but watch the tip of my tail' and you would see the last inch or so give an occasional twitch. Or it would move slowly and gently from side to side. This meant 'I am not asleep and I know what is going on'. An extension of this same movement to about three inches meant either 'leave me alone I want to go to sleep' or 'any more of this and I shall become angry'.

A full movement of the tail indicated 'I am angry' or 'I feel randy'. When the hunt was on the tail remained perfectly still, and like the tail of a pointer dog stood out horizontally, providing balance when the final pounce was made.

It is the same with all cats of course except the Manx, who, poor fellow, has to find other ways of expressing his feelings.

To say that Tigger was an exceptional cat seems hardly necessary. When talking to him and meeting that unwinking gaze from his big pleading eyes, and watching the almost imperceptible forward body movements one could be convinced he understood everything being said. He would open his mouth and give an almost soundless yak-yak.

His reactions reminded me of those of a stricken human unable to speak yet understanding all that was said. It was the body language of sheer frustration. He loved human company and tried to join in everything which might be going on.

If one took time to talk softly and sweetly to him, getting down to his level he would after a time, begin to purr.

Our guests, so far as he was concerned, were welcome providing they provided a lap and he was given a tid-bit if they were eating. He played cards, helped in the kitchen with the cooking and was always in attendance when I was at my desk writing. In fact he insisted on being part of the household and there were times, when getting in the way as he did Claire would say to him 'why can't you behave more like a cat?'

It was a while before the implications of that remark came home to us. It was, I suppose, indicative of how Tigger had got under our skins. I reminded Claire of those lines from Professor Higgins in Bernard Shaw's *Pygmalion* when he says to Eliza Dolittle 'why can't women be more like men?'

But Tigger *was* different. He seemed less afraid of humans than of his fellow species, about whom he was a bit of a coward. He avoided conflict simply because of his size and formidable manner. He could look a picture of menace but, had an aspiring contestant approached him, Tigger would have gone running

You perhaps have come to the conclusion that he was not a real cat at all. But there were many times when he behaved in that enchanting and loving way ordinary cats will do.

We used to play together with bits of paper folded into spills but most of all he loved his feather. This was kept on a low table and I have watched him out of the corner of my eye when I have been busy typing. He would sit and look at me for a while, then realising I was not going to play with him, would wander off to the low table and his feather. He would reach up, standing on his haunches to do so, knock it off, and amuse himself by throwing the feather up in the air and catching it.

One of the games which Tigger played regularly when we lived in the chalk cottage was 'the retreat' as we called it. When Claire went to the end of the long garden to hang out the washing or do some gardening he would follow her. He would wait around until she was about to return and set off down the lawn, waiting until she had gone a little ahead of him, then he would set off on a thundering charge at terrific speed his dainty little feet pounding on the ground. Having reached the house he would sit in the doorway waiting for her with an expression much as to say 'where the blazes have you been?' He knew it was a game because he would follow if we again walked up the garden and would repeat the whole process over again.

This need to be with us extended to wanting to be with us when we were bathing or shaving and when we used the WC he sat outside waiting for us to emerge.

Some people already know about the folk-law surrounding black cats A black cat without the saving grace of a few white hairs on its chest is still committed to the Community of Witches but not so many know how to detect which Tabbies are still committed to the Sorcerer's Coven. These are the servants of Merlin the Magician and are a line above black cats in the hierarchy.

It was not until Claire and I were discussing all this with some visiting friends and one of them said 'it *is* only a cat you know!' that we realised how close we had become to being paranoiac about him.

It was this remark which got me wondering if a cat could be a schizophrenic. Perhaps this was the reason for his bad temper which he exhibited for no particular reason. On more than one occasion he had nipped a ladies ankle and it seemed the prettier and the slimmer the less he could resist a nip.

Can a cat have a sense of humour? All animals, especially when very young, have a sense of fun but a sense of humour? Well we thought so. As I described, there were many times when he behaved in the enchanting and loving way ordinary cats will do. I'm sure we've all met those irritating annoying people with whom we feel we cannot spend any more time, then suddenly, they, like the King of Siam 'do something wonderful' and you forgive them. This was Tigger. Was he the King of Siam? Claire pondered one day.

Eleven pm was Tigger's bed time … at least *he* thought so, and went to the bottom of the stairs waiting for us and for his few moments of fun and the ritual of playing with his feather through the crack of the door.

He was not allowed to sleep in the bedroom but slept in a cardboard box lined with a blanket, outside the bedroom door.

Although a cat-flap had been provided for Tigger's use to use whenever he felt inclined, for whatever purpose, he seemed reluctant to use it and had developed the habit of scratching at the door indicating he wanted us to open it for him.

Sometimes he simply used his dirt tray rather than go outside the house. Only later did it occur to us that the top of the cat-flap might be hurting his back.

I felt Claire had, before my arrival in the household, indulged Tigger and it would now be difficult to break the habit. Whilst it was not a great inconvenience during the day the scratching on the bedroom door, either in the middle of the night or early morning asking to be let out, became a real nuisance.

We came to the conclusion that another cat introduced into the household which used the cat-flap might encourage or shame Tigger into doing likewise. So … realising that to bring in an adult cat after having let Tigger rule the roost for so long would almost certainly lead to friction we found a delightful little kitten named Barney.

From the similarity in their markings Barney could have been Tigger's son. And this seemed all the more a possibility in the way in which Tigger accepted this ball of mischief.

From the moment he arrived Barney began to boss Tigger around and Tigger did nothing whatever to retaliate. Barney gave him no peace.

He jumped and leapt around him and nipped his tail. He deliberately bumped into him knocking him off balance reducing Tigger's dignity no end. He demonstrated his affection in the most boisterous way succeeding only in making Tigger's life one long striving after peace and quiet.

Those of my readers who have had their young grandchildren dumped upon them for a day or two whilst the parents 'had a little rest' will know what I am talking about.

Barney needs no description for the photograph tells all.

Whenever Tigger walked Barney was there nipping his tail and his hindquarters causing Tigger's progress to be one of little spurts every time he was nipped. Tired of this, Barney would run around Tigger from the front tripping him up and waving his bottom in Tigger's face and flicking his tail in his eyes.

We watched in amazement as Tigger went his quiet unruffled way for it was not in his nature to be so acquiescent. His refuge was his stool in the kitchen which Barney could not reach.

Like the cardboard box outside the bedroom door Tigger had a similar one in the kitchen, it was his pride and joy … until Barney arrived! Barney was given a box of his own but he was not satisfied with that and proceeded to develop a system of infiltration which any Politician, General or thief would have been proud of.

The process began with Barney approaching Tigger in his box. Tigger. probably anticipating what was to come. would pretend to be asleep, and would settle down even more firmly and solidly and one could imagine him saying to himself 'this time I will *not* give way' … 'this time I will *not* give up this lovely box'.

But like all cats, once embarked upon a specific line of action he was not to be deterred. The process began with Barney approaching Tigger in his box from the outside.

Barney would gently wash Tigger's ears and head. This seemed to sooth Tigger who's eyes, if one watched closely, would begin to close even more firmly. Waiting for the appropriate moment, Barney would move around the open front of the box and begin a more general washing process placing first one front paw and then another very softly in the box.

Eventually he had insinuated himself totally into the box by sitting very quietly and gently on Tigger's legs. This caused Tigger to withdraw a little, a move which Barney immediately took advantage.

At this stage the pretence of washing stopped and in the small amount of space available Barney would sit up demurely for a short while, almost convincing one that he was 'guarding the old boy whilst he's asleep'. But very gradually he would spread himself until finally he was lying in the curve of Tigger's stomach or around his back.

This was the 'frontal approach' as Claire called it. There was not really room in the box for two and the early stages appeared innocent enough with Barney hanging all four feet over the edge, as if to give Tigger room, or perhaps, not to take up too much room. But gradually the pressure was increased with Tigger having to raise his head in order to avoid Barney's back. Tigger, in self defence, would make one or two half hearted attempts to push Barney out with his back legs but such efforts were useless until finally Tigger was obliged to sit up. This was the signal for Barney to take over the box by a quick wriggle and a back movement. Tigger would give up jump out of the box and go find himself another place to sleep peacefully.

If Tigger was lying face inwards in the box the technique of possession changed. Barney would lean over the side of the box and vigorously wash

Last time she offered me a dead mouse *he* had caught. This smells better.

I only do this to amuse her.

Tigger dressing for dinner.

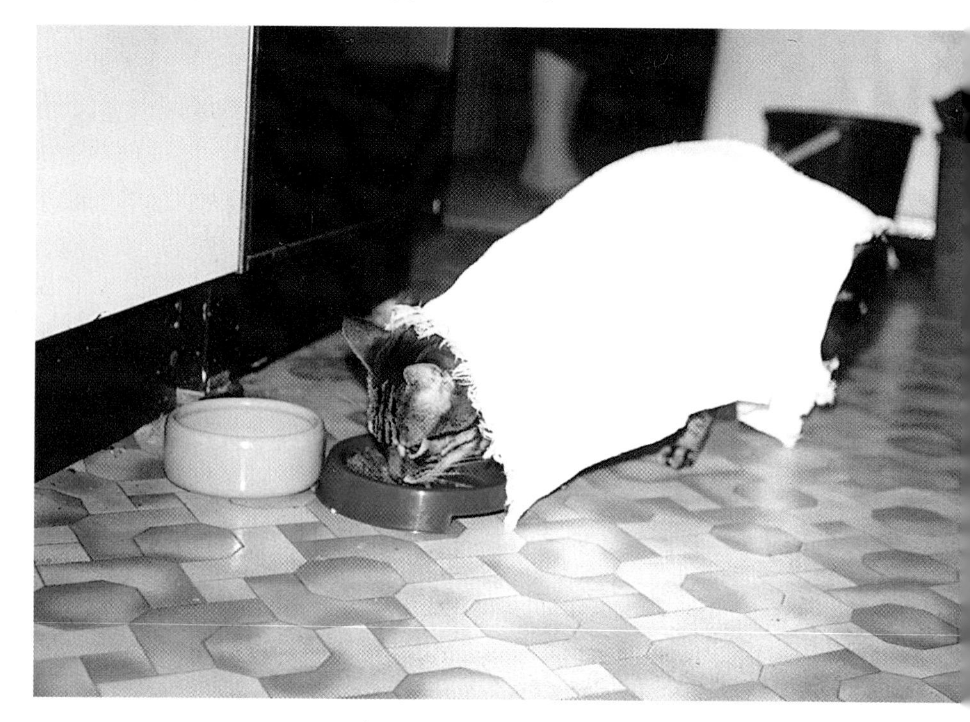

Tigger … dressed for dinner.

Tigger enjoying meat and two veg.

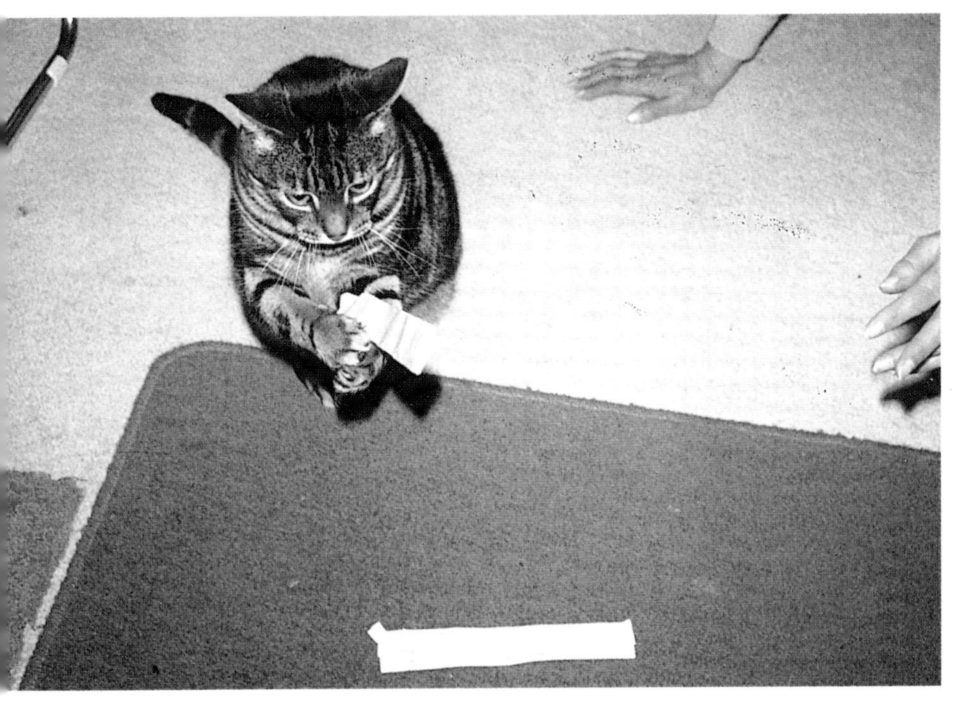

Tigger getting his paper slip to play with. (page 69).

Life is *so* boring.

Puss in Boots.

id you say “two spades”?’(page 69)

Cat-Cat watching snooker on TV.

Haven't I heard that one before?

Fritz – desperate for water showing signs of his kidney problem (page 6

He's gone – must be time for lunch.

Wake up! Its time for lunch. (page 58)

Tigger in a somewhat undignified situation.

Gimme … Gimme … Gimm

La Petit Chatte in Jersey. T
much travelled French lady.
(page 23)

The wino.

I wonder if they'll come and feed whilst I'm here.

Tigger in his box hoping Barney will leave him in peace (page 71).

Barney preparing for mischief (page 71).

I really can't believe there's someone else as beautiful as me.

Is this the pose you want? I like to look my best always.

THE SEDUCTION

See page 70

3
4

'Gad … that was a good night last night!

CAT the marmoset cat. (page 75).

Charlie taking his morning drink (page 78).

Tigger's head. This was done with such enthusiasm Tigger's head would wobble all over the place until finally he was given no alternative but to shift position. Barney's leap over the back of the box into the small space created by Tigger's move was timed to the second. From then on the process was swift and merciless. Barney replaced Tigger simply by adopting the position Tigger has so meekly abandoned, and it was only a moment or two before Tigger was pushed through the open front.

Why Tigger put up with this persecution we could never fathom. It was not that Barney really wanted the box for no sooner had he obtained possession than he was out of it thinking up some game he might persuade Tigger to play.

One day Barney failed to return from one of his sorties. From the day of his arrival he had made full use of the wide open spaces surrounding the cottage. It was farming country, and as might be expected traps, both illegal and legal had been installed everywhere. Combine Harvesters worked the fields. Farmers shot rabbits.

Claire believed Barney had been scooped up by one of these but I argued he was far too agile to be caught by one of those. Much more likely he had been shot or had been caught in a gin trap. To add to our speculation Claire had seen some Travellers a few fields away. Here again I argued it was unlikely they would have kept him for his fur. He was too small. Certainly he might have just left home and joined them but this seemed the least of the possibilities.

Barney did not return. For a while Tigger once more ruled the roost in Claire's house but we *had* noticed an improvement in Tigger's use of the cat-flap so, once more we set about finding a cat which might be acceptable to Tigger.

In a matter of weeks we had acquired Cindy. We had heard through a friend that they knew of someone who was going abroad and wanted a home for their cat.

One visit to meet Cindy and we needed no persuasion to adopt her. She was quite a large black and white neutered female, with a longish loose coat, a beautiful black tail and even markings, a white chest and socks and a short black 'jacket' on her back. The black blob which had 'slid' over her left eye gave her appearance a 'fashionable' twist.

What struck us most however was the air of nonchalance and calm assumption that everything was her right. She had that air of the aristocrat expecting everything to go her way without making the effort.

This became immediately apparent when we got her home. To our surprise she took over without any protest from Tigger. Gentleman, as he was, he gave her pride of place before the fire, and stood aside when they were fed whilst she chose her eating bowl. He guarded her.

Her participation in fun and games was restrained and ladylike and she rarely spoke.

Being accustomed only to living previously in a flat, the realisation, having found the cat-flap, that there was a big wild world available to her came as a cultural shock.

In no time at all she was going where Tigger had feared to tread. Despite her sojourns into the hay barn nearby; her fishing in the pond for the goldfish; the tree climbing after the birds which teased her endlessly, she never lost her air of calm superiority.

I wondered how many other cat owners had had the good fortune to have two such remarkable cats.

We moved house and they came with us … a cat in each car in their cat boxes. A car crash involving both cars on the way to our new home left them and us unharmed.

Both cats settled down happily in their new home but, sadly, it was not to last for Claire received an urgent call from her relations in Australia. The trouble, apparently, was serious. Not knowing how long she would be away the house was closed up and I had to find temporary accommodation and the cats were given to her son and daughter to care for.

I missed them terribly. Neither were cats which would find settling down with a new master and mistress that easy, and whilst Claire seemed content with what she had arranged, I felt they would not have been understood as we had understood them.

As it turned out I never saw either of those cats again.

Claire decided to stay in Australia and once more I had to start planning my life and my future.

Chapter Twelve

CAT AND CHARLIE

Supportive friends in North Wales offered me a temporary haven which I gratefully accepted … besides they had a really beautiful cat. And as I have already said in times of stress, trouble and sadness, cats have been my sympathetic and understanding companions.

Cat was beautiful. A neutered female she was truly a Queen.

I was immediately struck by her unusual markings which for a cat, were remarkably symmetrical. She wore a cap of pale fawn and gold with a central peak of black streaks between the ears. The lower part of her face was white setting off a pretty little pink nose. Her chest, forelegs and shoulders were encased in pure white and at the back of each white foreleg was a cuff of pale fawn markings matching her 'jacket' of brown grey with dark stripes running around her body. Her tail was long and ringed turning from light brown colouring at the base to a black tip. As I looked at her fascinated, I realised that her markings and colourings were those of a marmoset … even to the reddish brown tinting on her head.

I commented on this to my friends. They admitted to not having taken particular notice except to appreciate that she was beautifully marked. They went to their encyclopaedia to find that I was not mistaken. There it was before us … a cat and a monkey with the same markings.

Needless to say from then on the discussion raged as to how a cat could come to have markings similar to a monkey with such primeval ancestry. I confess we failed to arrive at a satisfactory explanation.

Apparently Cat loved ping-pong (sorry! table tennis) balls. Thrown on the floor she would dash after one and knock it around the room like a football, first with one paw then the other, and at times lifting it up with both front paws, throwing it in the air and knocking it with a paw before it reached the ground. She was a hunter and this was obvious by the wriggle of her bottom before she pounced on a ball.

A ping-pong ball was part of her pre-bedtime play time. A ritual which had to be gone through most nights. My friends would stand at the top of the stairs with a handful of balls whilst Cat sat beside them waiting her head tilted upwards towards them with an expectant look on her face.

My friends would then let a ball begin to bounce from the top stair downwards, stair by stair. As soon as this began to happen Cat was alert and watching intently. The game, which both we and she understood, was for her to catch the ball before it reached the bottom.

She rarely failed to time her scramble down the stairs to catch the ball when it had reached half way. 'With a flick of her paw she would send the ball into the hallway tumbling helter-skelter down the rest of the stairs to chase the ball wherever it may have run.

Cat, having completed one 'run' returned to the top of the stairs to go through the whole performance again and again until one side or the other got tired.

Beneath the stairs there were small doors providing access to the understairs. The larger area had been turned into a cupboard but a small section near the bottom was not used … except by Cat … when she would open the small door and go to sleep inside.

We began to get worried when we noticed a distinct falling off in her activities. She became listless wanting to do nothing but sleep and eating little. She drank large quantities of water and of milk, but this seemed not to help. She became so ill my friends took her to the Vet who confessed to being nonplussed as to what could be wrong. X-Rays revealed nothing, not even a fur ball. From being so impeccably groomed she became spikey and ceased to wash herself.

Finally the Vet traced her illness to respiration but tests again revealed nothing. He then started asking about her diet. Where had she been hunting? What was her diet? Was she eating any plants or flowers in the field at the back of the house? Was anyone else feeding her? Had she been hunting? Did she eat what she caught? Were there any rats in the neighbourhood? Where was she sleeping?

Poor Cat she had been getting worse and worse and was, by now in something near to a coma. Crawling away to her hide-e-hole. We were all frantic with worry.

Then suddenly … the penny dropped. Where she was sleeping there were the gas meters. Just recently the gas engineers had been round to make some adjustments to the position of the meters. My friend crawled inside. Cat's bed of old towels was close by the meters and in that small confined space there was a trace of a smell of gas.

From then on everything went into top gear. The Gas Company was contacted and engineers came racing to deal with the leak. Cat was rushed off to the Vet and told of the turn of events. He gave her an injection. He instructed us to feed her alternatively with water and milk from a dropper every hour, right through the night.

For the first forty-eight hours there seemed no improvement except that she accepted her droplets of liquid without protest. From then on progress was swift and within a fortnight Cat was almost her old self again.

With time to think not one of us could imagine how we had not smelled the gas leak and congratulated ourselves that there had been no explosion Cat had probably saved us from fire or worse.

Helping to look after Cat had been a wonderful therapy for me. My own troubles had attained a new dimension and my frequent talks with Cat had helped to heal my sadness.

Much as I loved Cat and much as my friends made me welcome beyond the bounds of friendship I had to think about finding a place of my own.

In due course I rented a house in the same town, moved in and settled down to write.

The house, at the end of the street, had a wonderful view across the River Dee and to the Wirral and across the road was the Recreation Ground.

Twenty yards to my right was a row of shops the nearest one to me being a Fried Fish shop. The owners of the shop were my next door neighbours, a delightful young couple who welcomed my arrival, invited me into tea, and introduced me to Charlie.

Charlie was big. Charlie was immediately friendly and his welcoming purring was balm to my emotional bruises.

I had not been there a week when on opening the back door I found Charlie waiting patiently. I invited him in, not that he needed any invitation for as soon as the door was open he walked casually in turning to look at me, as much as to say 'got any milk?' Of course he got some.

He ignored the food I provided strolled across the room and took up position in a large comfortable black leather armchair in the dining room.

Charlie was a ginger/white combination with a marking distribution not unlike that of Cat even to the slightly ringed tail. He had the white waistcoat, the white forelegs and a ginger cap over a white face. One of his most endearing habits was the way in which he allowed the very tip of a pink tongue to peep from his mouth.

With all that lovely fish available every day from his master and mistress he was not interested in food. Finally, his early morning visits became a daily habit. I had no cat-flap so I was obliged, on getting up, to go straight down to the back door to let him in, leaving the door open.

Once or twice he came upstairs into my bedroom but never stayed long preferring his leather chair. I think he must have been aware what an excellent background the black leather made for his white and ginger colouring

When I was working at the sink preparing myself a meal or washing up after one, Charlie was there and no sooner had I finished than he would be on to the draining board and into the sink lapping up the remaining water, or, if I allowed the tap to run directly drinking from the tap.

Every afternoon as a break from my work at the desk I would go across to the Recreation Ground for a walk around. I needed the fresh air and exercise.

Just occasionally I would meet Charlie on the Ground when we would exchange greetings but, unlike so many cats, he never felt it necessary to accompany me. We were very often the only two there.

With only a one year lease I was sad when I was given notice to leave because the owner wished to resume residence. This meant another move, this time to the South Coast where I found a flat a few hundred yards from the beach near Selsey Bill.

Two or three years after leaving my house and Charlie I was once more in North Wales. I 'dropped in' to say 'hello' to my friendly neighbours and ask after Charlie for he had meant a great deal to me during my moments of unhappiness whilst I was there.

Asking after Charlie I was told he had died about a year after I had left. It was apparently severe kidney trouble.

It was then I realised that Charlie's constant demand for fluids ... water and milk ... must have signalled the earlier symptoms of his kidney trouble.

I was sad for him and hoped he had not suffered too much in the last stages of his illness. Why, I chastised myself, had I not with the knowledge and experience of Fritz recognised the symptoms in Charlie?

He had never been a cat to cuddle, nor to rub against one's legs or jump on one's lap, nor had he ever spent a night with me on my bed and I wondered if this avoidance of being handled was because he suffered pain when touched. He had been my constant companion and someone to say 'good morning' to every morning without fail whilst I was there.

Charlie was the last cat with whom I had any lengthy companionship and since then my cat meetings have been casual and short lived such as encounters in the street or in friends houses.

That then completes the tales of the cats in my life.

* * *

After a few years I moved to live in the country.

Of course there have been 'incidents' where cats were involved. There was the occasion when I was called to rescue a cat which had become entangled in a gin-trap planted in a hedge. The poor thing, not unlike Fritz, a big black tom, back legs entangled, was flailing around suspended by the wires in great pain. Freeing him from this murderous contraption was not easy. I wrapped him in a blanket took him home gave him milk, examined him to find his injuries and was surprised to find how light they were. I dressed them and allowed him to sleep it off. Later that day I let him go after a hearty meal to report his adventure to his owner.

I never did find out who he belonged to or saw him again.

Then there was the occasion of the milk bottles. Quite suddenly we had a spate of upturned milk bottles with the tops torn off. At first this was thought to be the work of some big bird, but an early morning vigil proved differently.

The mother cat who came to steal the milk was ginger and white. Rather like a female version of Charlie but much smaller. She knocked the milk bottle over, tore the top off and called her three kittens in to 'sup up'. Further investigation revealed the fact that she was a stray who had decided to use one of our sheds to have her kittens and now they were grown a little she was teaching them how to fend for themselves.

All three kittens were really beautiful. I submitted to their charms and began feeding the family. They were wild. They were nervous and would only eat when I moved back into the house. Then, one day the kittens arrived for their meal without Mum. Mum, it turned out later, had been run over. The kittens were on their own. I continued to feed them but they would still not come near me peeping from around the side of a shed in the garden with one little head about the other, eyes bright, wide open and fearful.

Finally we contacted the local Cats Protection League from whom I borrowed cages. After a difficult and complicated plan I eventually persuaded them, fighting and spitting, into the cages, and took them to The Ludlow C.P.L. Shop.

I later heard they had all found good homes. I really regretted not keeping the beautiful tortoiseshell for he was undoubtedly the prize of the three.

Perhaps now is the time to stop telling stories about *my* cats and let you hear about other people's cats.

TRUE STORIES ABOUT CATS WITH NINE LIVES

From 'ALL GOD'S CREATURES' by Sister Seraphim

'Then there was Tom, the famous Cathedral cat whose carved image now gazes out from the top of a pillar in St. James's Chapel, but who lived, loved and hunted and haunted the aisles in the wake of the head verger.

The cat and I became great friends and when he saw me, he invariably trotted over and settled down on the seat next to me. Since he could be considered part of the Cathedral staff my father was not embarrassed by Tom's company.

'The cat did most of the talking. He told me what he thought of the dog. "He's quite the gentleman, I'm glad to see. I watched him carefully for the first few days when he came here. Had he misbehaved he'd be minus an eye by now."

'I had no difficulty in understanding cat talk or in making cats understand me. Had it been the middle of the 17th century I might have been branded a witch.'

Sister Seraphim also tells of the outrageous story of the cat which insisted upon sleeping on the open pages of the Gospel on the Chapel altar.

Sister Seraphim is a Devonian turned Russian Orthodox Nun. Her love of animals, another St. Francis, her love of cats in particular, runs through her book like a golden thread. 'All God's Creatures' was published by William Kimber and Co. Ltd., of London in 1975.

A MOVE TOO FAR?
Territorial Rights

It is well known that the cat is one of the species of animals which mark out their territory when young and guard it jealously.

Many of us when moving house and take along our pet cat have noticed, in certain circumstance, how the cat will immediately set about marking out its territory by spraying, and, if there are other cats in the neighbourhood especially nearby how for a period of time there is contention where the *established* cat resents having to give up part of what was *its* territory to the newcomer.

I have known cases where an incoming cat will become almost a prisoner in the house – its new home, venturing out only when nature calls or at night.

The story of Pilsbury is most unusual.

It all began with his 'owners' (one almost hesitates to use such a word) moving eight miles from their home in Backwell, Bristol to a village called Yatton.

Pilsbury was eight years old and his family had been in Backwell for eighteen years. He had arrived in Backwell as a kitten.

It was not long before Geoff French and his daughter had reason to worry about Pilsbury's absence. He was away days and distracted Sarah had almost given up hope when their former neighbour in Backwell, Beryl Hockin, phoned Sarah to say Pilsbury was sitting in their drive. His journey had taken four days.

So for Sarah and Geoff it was off to Backwell to bring him back looking a little forlorn but fit and well.

Back in the new house in Yatton Pilsbury just sat around, subdued and not like the cat they knew in Bristol. He had not been there much more than a week when once more he vanished, and once more after a few days Beryl Hockin phoned to say he was back in Backwell clean and uninjured.

Pilsbury had made the eight mile journey across main roads, streams, open country and avoiding stray dogs and feral cats on the way, feeding on the wild life.

Pilsbury when we went to press, had done the journey an amazing 40 times travelling a total of 320 miles. Making the journey almost weekly and being brought back by Sarah and Geoff, each time.

The story of Pilsbury is remarkable in that there appears to be no known equal and gives rise to speculation as to the *real* reason why he determinedly returned to his original home.

In Backwell he was undoubtedly Top Cat but in Yatton there was some doubt. Having been Top Cat in Backwell was he meeting opposition from Yatton cats with established territories?

Animal Behaviour expert Peter Neville when told of the story said 'a cat's livelihood depends on its territory. To return eight miles is most unusual … a mile or so is not so unusual but *eight miles*!!

The syndrome of returning to one's 'roots' is not unusual in human beings. The feeling of restlessness in many people when, for whatever reason, even holidays, they are anxious to return to their familiar surroundings. Some need to return for a token visit, others find the pull so strong they return to live there.

Understanding this which, perhaps Geoff French did not, when I moved cats I kept them for a short period in the house, allowing them to mark this territory first then later putting them on a lead and letting them mark their outer perimeters.

My mother used to suggest putting butter on the cat's paws believing this would remove the smell of their old haunts as they licked the butter off.

Pilsbury is famous now for his story appeared on Television.

There is a colour picture of Pilsbury in this book facing page 73.

THE PIOUS CAT

When the Rev. Stephen Cawley moved with his wife from Birkenhead to be Vicar of St. Mary's Church at Broughton, North Wales they brought with them their four cats.

Tigger, who was five at the time, and whom they had adopted as a kitten had already established himself in Birkenhead as 'top cat'.

He had already demonstrated a distinct religious leaning in Birkenhead. In the Vicarage in Broughton, he once more began attending choir practice in St. Mary's Church.

Of the various ceremonies held in the Church his favourite was Evensong, which he attended regularly, but did become restless if the sermon went on too long.

Soon after his arrival with the Rev. Cawley he was, when attending an annual general meeting, invited to become an honorary member of the Church Council. His behaviour on all these occasions was impeccable restraining himself from interrupting the proceedings and restricting comment to loud sonorous purrs.

But there was one event when his love of comfort overcame his usual gentlemanly behaviour. This is how it was told to me verbatim by the Rev. Cawley.

'Tigger came to Evensong as usual on Easter Day where, the sermon being short, he was good as gold throughout the whole service. Unfortunately, he chose to sit in the same pew as a lady who was suffering from piles, and who used a special cushion to ease the discomfort. During the singing of the psalm Tigger discovered her cushion and appropriated it for the rest of the service, leaving her to perch very uncomfortably on the edge of the seat. I must say she was remarkably good-humoured about it.'

That was in 1989.

When in the process of compiling this book we again contacted the Rev. Cawley he had moved to become the Vicar of the Parishes of Gwernsffield and Llanferres in Mold, North Wales, and had of course taken Tigger along too.

That was in October 1997.

In no time at all Tigger, now 17, went missing.

Tigger was missing for a fortnight and the Rev.Cawley and his wife spent many frantic days and nights spreading the news of his disappearance through the Parishes.

Then one evening there was a phone call from Mrs Ada Leneham who came from Cadole, about three miles away, to say she had found Tigger. Mrs Leneham who worked in Gwernsffield had met Tigger before he went missing and had recognised him.

Slowly Tigger is being encouraged to adopt his old habits of attending Evensong but he seems still to retain a desire to wander.

Author's note:

Is this yet another example of a cat wanting his old haunts, as with Pilsbury? (See story 'A move too far' page 83.)

Pilsbury travelled eight miles and knew where he wanted to go but Tigger, if he wanted to go back to Broughton had gone in the wrong direction. Broughton is 10 miles east of Gwernsffield and Cadole is three miles west.

For a cat to go in the wrong direction is unusual.

Perhaps Tigger was unhappy with his new territory. Perhaps the area had already been marked out by other cats already well established, and he knew he would not be able to establish himself there without a fight, so he was looking for an easier area.

Tigger at 17 no doubt wants a quieter life and the thought of starting life again in Gwernsffield was too much to contemplate.

If poor Tigger had wanted to return to Broughton he would have had not only a long journey but a very difficult one, much more difficult than that experienced by Pilsbury, who was only eight and … as they would say in the 'Eastenders' 'a little more streetwise' than Tigger.

WANDERER RETURNS: The Rev. Stephen Cawley with his roaming cat Tigger.

'FLOORED BUT NOT OUT'

Tessie was a six year old black cat and she had been missing for two weeks. Her family had been going frantic throughout that time, asking neighbours if they had seen her and had been out every night and day calling her name.

Julian, Helen Parton's two year old son was heart-broken and they had almost given up hope when during a final search Mr Parton Senior (Bill) and Julian heard meowing from a partially built house next door.

Tracking down the noise to a room with freshly laid floor boards they found her there.

How Tessie survived the two weeks in the dark without food or water is one of those mysteries with which we associate the ability of cats to survive. Tessie was thin and bedraggled but after careful nursing and a visit to the vet for a check up she is now back to normal and recounting her experiences with Mrs Parton's other cat Fluffy.

Perhaps, if Tessie had had the required six white hairs on her chest she would have been luckier … on the other hand, as she was still a Witches' companion, perhaps the Witches looked after her.

With acknowledgements the *Shropshire Star* for the original story

A CAT IN A WASHING MACHINE

Barney, a little black kitten was the Chiu family's favourite pet, but like lots of pets in lots of families where there are young children, he was always in danger of becoming the subject of some innocent childish prank.

Poor Barney got the surprise of his short young life when three-year-old Sophie Chiu popped him into the washing machine and set it going. He was drenched, spun and rinsed for 15 minutes before Sophie ran to tell her mother Claire that 'Barney is in the washing machine' … 'He's going round and round'.

Mrs Chiu rushed into the kitchen and in her panic pushed the wrong button and instead of stopping it set it off on a high-speed spin dry! Quickly she pulled the plug from the wall and rescued Barney.

At the vets where Barney was immediately taken he was patched up and put on a drip. To everyone's relief Barney made a full recovery with his already natural dislike of water now firmly enhanced.

The vet had a sense of humour for when Barney was taken back later for a check up he said 'I can give him a clean bill of health'.

With acknowledgements to the *Shropshire Star*

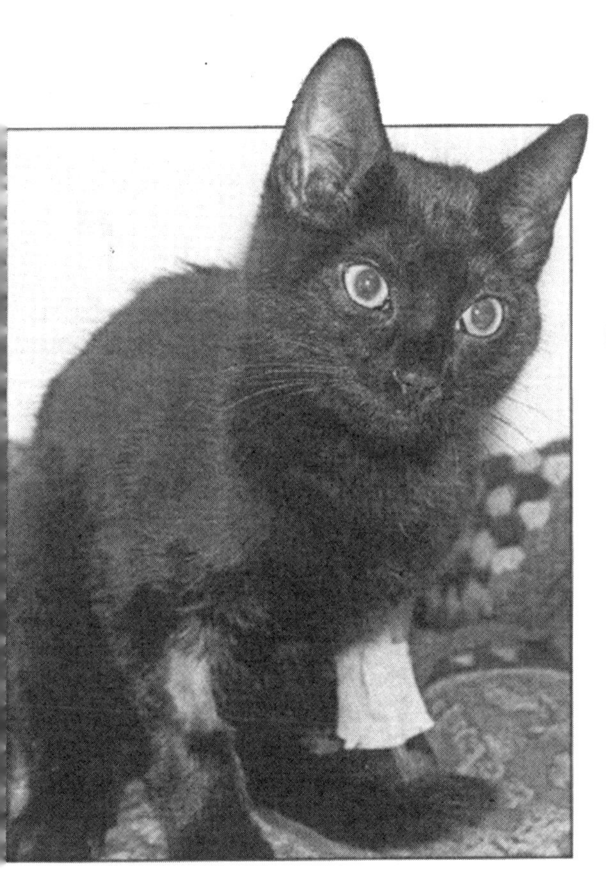

SOMETHING TO THINK ABOUT

In 1986 Golden Wonder Crisps put the following 'joke' on the side of their packets of Wotsits snacks.

Q: 'What's small, fluffy and goes round and round?'
A: 'A kitten in a washing machine!'

In 1988, eighteen months later, three year old Sophie Chiu put her kitten Barney in the washing machine (see story on page 90) but it is highly unlikely that there is any connection between the two events, for the Company ceased printing that particular joke on their packets once it had been pointed out how unsuitable it was. Also, little Sophie was only eighteen months old at the time.

Jane Green a member of the Cats Protection League in Atherstone Warwickshire, spotted the 'joke' and complained to the Company. Production of the packets was stopped.

In their defence the company explained that before printing the 'jokes' 100 of them had been presented to children between ages six to eleven. This was one of the 24 to be chosen.

What the Company did not explain was how many children were invited to make their choices.

One is tempted to question the wisdom of relying on the judgement of children for such action especially over such a wide range of ages. A child of eleven has a different outlook from that of one of six. What is acceptable or unacceptable to one may be abhorrent or frightening to the other.

One is also tempted to question whether the 'joke' was the invention of a child or an adult. We suspect an adult created it believing it would have a 'funny' connotation for a child. And had that adult an already established attitude of little concern for acts of cruelty towards animals?

We have included this story as it highlights the need for unceasing vigilance by everyone who cares for animals and to take action whenever irresponsible adults with little concern for animals use them for commercial 'knock about'.

The story overleaf confirms that there was no need to 'plant' the idea in any child's mind for surely it was there already?

BUTTON THE SURVIVOR

How long can a cat live without without food and little water?

As most cat owners will acknowledge, cats love to explore; they are inquisitive and will sometimes spread their investigations a considerable distance from their homes.

Button, a four year old Ginger persian-cross was no exception.

Builders, Pelham Homes of Norwich, working on a new estate in Balderton, Newark, Nottinghamshire had got as far as laying a suspended concrete floor to a garage.

Before it was finished Button, unnoticed by the workmen managed to squeeze into a 6 inch aperture before the floor was sealed up, convinced no doubt, there was something special beneath requiring her attention.

When Button didn't return after a day or two, for she was often away for such periods, Jamie Boness, her owner began to worry. Night after night day after day he and his girlfriend went out calling her name and asking neighbours if they had seen her, but all without success.

Jamie and his girlfriend were distraught as days became weeks and they spread their search in an increasingly wide circle around their home.

Neighbours close to where the garage had been built had been puzzled by meowing. Tracing it to the garage they opened the door but found nothing whilst still hearing the meowing which became louder and more insistent when Button, undoubtedly heard their voices.

The yeowling continued so they called in the RSPCA.

Once at the site, realising he could do nothing RSPCA Officer called in the fire brigade who arrived with a thermal imaging camera – the kind used to find people buried beneath collapsed buildings – and there, sure enough after a lengthy and careful scan, was the expected 'reaction'.

Immediately excavations began at the foundations and after 7 hours a weak, bedraggled and very thin Button emerged.

Mr Ian Callagham said in all his 19 years he had never come across anything quite like this. Button had survived for three and a half weeks in complete blackness with only the dampness of the clay floor and perhaps some earth worms to eat. But she was rescued only just in time Mr Callagham believes.

Neil Burnett, the building manager, who was there during the rescue operation said had the search not been successful he was prepared to rip up the garage to save Button.

Button, who had lost 4lb during her ordeal is now fully recovered and back exploring.

Postscript: 'Is this perhaps a case where curiosity almost killed the cat?

As columnist Nigel Nicholson once remarked 'is it not strange that a cat should be supposedly blessed with nine lives yet sacrifice that ninth life because of curiosity?'

Curiosity keeps us mentally alert there is no doubt, so why be surprised that a cat is curious and mentally alert? My father taught me never to stop asking 'Why?' Is that, I sometimes wonder, why I love cats?

GIZMO THE FLYING CAT*

Perhaps Gizmo had never heard of the famous Tigger who was always getting into situations from which he could not extricate himself, or was he just trying to go one better?

Whatever persuaded him to go 60 foot up a tree no one will ever know but once up he certainly could not get down, and let everyone know in no uncertain terms.

Someone heard his pitiful cries and called the firebrigade. So in came the fire-brigade with hydraulic platform to Castlecroft Road, near the Castlecroft House Hotel.

Gizmo had worked himself up into such a state that when the platform was raised to rescue him he just fled to the end of a long branch.

By this time the road had been closed for two hours so the firefighters decided to saw the branch down and catch him in a sheet, but the branch was rotten snapped and hurled Gizmo into space to fall 60 feet.

Believe it or not Gizmo just walked away seemingly oblivious of the chaos he had created and without a word of thanks to those who had come to rescue him.

With acknowledgements to the *Shropshire Star* for the original true story

*As shown on ITV Central in the 'Animal Rescuers' programme on Monday 20th July 1998

GIZMO The Flying cat.

MINNIE THE CLIFF HANGER

Would it not be interesting to learn how often the firebrigade is called out to rescue cats? In this little collection of stories the firebrigade was called out on four occasions.

If cats are not up trees, under floorboards, in motor cars they are up chimneys.

Minnie chose the latter, and believe it or not got stuck up there. Black and ginger when she went up and probably all black by the time she had got half way.

Six year old Scarlett Cliff heard the cat's meowing and told her mum Jill who alerted the firebrigade.

Using a fishing rod they tried to coax her out. That wasn't successful so they climbed onto the roof and freed her by pushing her out with a chimney rod after 45 minutes, not before having knocked a few bricks out to try to reach her from another point.

Once free Minnie ran off (was she ashamed at causing so much trouble?) but was soon back for a meal to restore her confidence.

She had already cleaned herself up ready to be seen in public once again in Havelock Road, Belle Vue, Shrewsbury.

With acknowledgements to the *Shropshire Star* for the original story

TAKEN FOR A RIDE

As everyone knows cats love the warmth of a car and the feeling of safety beneath when danger threatens, but one cat who was subsequently named Mac took the whole thing to the extreme when he settled himself down in the bonnet of a car.

Graham McCallion owner of a J-reg 5 series BMW had the surprise of his life when on opening the bonnet he saw something hanging from the bottom of the car.

He had just returned from a two day trip to Scotland and in the process had travelled at least 1500 miles.

As he looked it moved and he could see what appeared to be a cat's tail, yet he still couldn't believe it, there it was wedged in near the radiator.

Mr McCalliom of Wootton Bassett, Wiltshire, called in the assistance of his friend Mr Gary Watts, but even the efforts of this cat lover to extricate

the cat were unsuccessful so they called in the firebrigade. The tasty food offered, Mac rejected, so eventually a fireman courageously pulled the cat free braving the flailing claws.

The cat, who had been named Mac because of his 'Scottish' connections, was taken to Vet Bas Sheltenpool who on examination concluded Mac had been there two days without food or water.

Poor old Mac was in a bit of a state, starved, somewhat dehydrated and certainly suffering from shock plus a singe on his ear. He was given an injection to calm him down.

Cat lovers Mr Watts and his wife Jane think Mac is somewhere between three and six years old, but after this experience, if not much older then certainly a wiser cat.

Mac is now part of the Watts family which already incorporates two other rescued cats and they all seem to be getting on fine together.

In the meantime the RSPCA are attempting to trace Mac's owner. One wonders if Mac shows off to his friends boasting about his travels.

SOME CAT POEMS

A Dog is so noble but not very bright
He will wait curled up tight on a mat
To be led for a walk and locked up at night,
whereas, *I* make the rules … *I'm a Cat*!

M. Eyres

PANGUR BAN

I and Pangur Ban my cat,
'Tis a like task we are at:
Hunting mice is his delight,
Hunting words I sit all night.

Better far than praise of men
'Tis to sit with book and pen;
Pangur bears me no ill will,
He, too, plies his simple skill.

'Tis a merry thing to see
At our tasks how glad are we,
When at home we sit and find
Entertainment to our mind.

Oftentimes a mouse will stray
In the hero Pangur's way,
Oftentimes my keen thought set
takes a meaning in its net.

'Gainst the wall he sets his eye,
Full and fierce and sharp and sly:
'Gainst the wall of knowledge I
All my little wisdom try.

When a mouse darts from its den
Oh, how glad is Pangur then!
Oh, what gladness do I prove
When I solve the doubts I love.

Practice every day has made
Pangur perfect in his trade.
I get wisdom day and night,
Turning darkness into light.

So in peace our task we ply,
Pangur Ban my cat, and I;
In our arts we find our bliss,
I have mine and he has his.

(trans. by Robin Flower from
the 9th century Irish)

WHIZZER
by
Eileen Spencer Trott

We loved you very much.
Such is the stuff of our tears
Years ago you came to us
black and shiny, a present
for Matthew.

Soon you learnt to do 'paw',
Put your paw on our face
when we held you.
Not a miaow came from your mouth
for years.

You waited till we settled
in a fireside chair
then, bright-eyed, you were there,
quick onto a lap,
purring while we stroked you.

Dear Whizzer
for sixteen years
you have held our hearts,
making our family five.
Thank you for loving us.

(January 10th 1997)

CAT
by
Derek Harvey

Black parabola
Omniscient bulge
Almond opalescent eyes shuttered against the sun
refracting only the living darkness
Moon beast
You are pure Id.

In Medieval England they burnt you alive
'Room to swing a cat in' is more than a metaphor;
Our righteous ancestors called you 'the witches' handmaid'.
For women and cats represented the Devil
To metaphysical bishops
Afraid of the ranging body and its urging blood
Afraid
Of their own guts.
So you, spontaneously perversely alive, had to be the scapegoat.
You and some women with 'dark powers'.

And today Walt Disney has vilified you again
For the American public is afraid of you too –
Cat contra 20th Century Ego!

Cat in vignettes:
Delicately conscious black drop among the flower beds
Sniffing at the petals and nibbling
Dynamic coil
Polarising the peace of many a mellow wall
Inscrutably stretched-out sac
heavily spongeing in sun and fire

'Cat's Tales'

Quick shadow tangled in the no-man's land of upper architecture
Earth-drawn
Fire-fed.
Heartiness boastfulness work bustle
These you abhor;
Independence power exploration peace play meditation
Are your birthright.
Aristocrat of life
The crumbling West will pass like a bad smell
Long before you cease to hunt and purr.

With acknowledgements to the book 'People Within' (a collection of poetry)
published by The Thornhill Press

Lament of the Cats of Rapallo
(1st November 1972)
by
Ruthven Todd

We have our personal poetry
Of movement and of speech.
Our *Maiu* is *Miaow*
With different spellings.
Our gestures vary
But tonight our backs are turned
Against any gloating lights:
An old tradition hurts us all.

Sometimes we are silent. Our raw bones
Make sand-ripples of our draggled fur:
Our bellies rumble as our *maius* are muted,
Failing to explain our loss.

A long time since he went away –
The tall man with the red hair greying
And the beard tickling as he stooped
To give away a morsel. His "Puss-puss-puss",
In many languages, was his private voice
And all our ancestors knew him.
His pockets, still recalled in legend,
Were plump with scraps, regardless of the weather.

We, purring sadly to his memory, know well
He was a poet, for the once-hungry called
To the starving and spoke our way. Politicians
Have come and gone but none thought of us.

We are the shabby cats from the grimy alleys
Now in mourning. Our drum-tight skins
Reverberate with ancient memories
He was a poet as we ourselves are poets.
He spoke with gentle words, words
We did not really understand but meaningful.
We had hoped return
In his old gentleness.

We hear, as cats hear, that he is dead.

So tonight, if we call quietly in the lanes
We are not, as habitually, begging – but lamenting.
We, the cats of Rapallo, avoiding all the lights,
Ask only that our tribute to Ezra be recorded.

With acknowledgements to the book 'People Within' (a collection of poetry) published by The Thornhill Press

THE CATIOPAEDIA

THE CAT-TIONARY

ADAGES, APHORISMS AND APOTHEGMS

THE CATIOPAEDIA

CAT Is the term now commonly used to describe the domestic cat and its distant cousin the wild cat (see Wild Cat), although the term Cat is also correctly used still to describe any of the carnivorous mammals belonging to the Felidae family. The full company of the Cat family includes, Lions, Tigers, Pumas, Leopards, Panthers, Cheetahs, Jaguars, Lynx, Servals and Ocelots.

CAT (Domestic) There are various species of the domesticated cat, some of natural origins others the result of both accidental and careful breeding by Cat Fanciers These are the main varieties: Abyssinian; Asian; Bengal; Birman; British Shorthairs; Burmese; Chinchilla; Colourpoint; Cornish Rex; Cross breeds; Devon Rex; Exotic Shorthairs; Korats; Maine Coon; Manx; Norwegian Forest; Ocicats; Oriental; Persian; Ragdoll; Russian Blue; Scottish Fold; Siamese; Somali; Sphynx; Tortie Tabby; Tonkinese; Turkish Vans.

WILD CAT (British) Now found only in the Highlands of Scotland. Correct name: Felix Catus. Resembles the grey domestic cat but is bigger and heavier. Unpopular with farmers and game hunters because of its attacks on game, lambs and young deer. These wild cats and the European wild cat are rarely caught and are generally considered as being untameable.

WILD CAT (European) Correct name: Felis Sylvestris. Larger than the British wild cat averaging almost 3 feet long and somewhat different in colour being brownish/grey with a dark line along the back tail to head. Found almost all over Europe with the exception of the Alps, Apennines and Sicily.

Wild Cats in other parts of Europe, Asia and Africa are the Sardinian Wild Cat (Felis Sardia) which has a particularly long tail and tufts of hair at the tips of its pointed ears; the North African Wild Cat (Felis Libyca) similar to the Sardinian Wild Cat and the Central African Wild Cat (called Tiger Cat) Correct name (Profelia aurata) and the black footed cat of Southern Africa (Felis nigripea).

CAT HISTORY The most commonly known historical associations of the cat in history are with the Egyptians almost certainly because of their adoption of the Cat as the symbol of Bast the Goddess of Happiness and Maternity. (See pages 116 & 121.)

Around the same period, some 2000 years ago, writings in Sanskrit record the homage and esteem bestowed upon cats throughout India whilst it was a capital offence to kill a cat in Egypt.

Cats were also chosen as sacred objects in Burma where they were kept in the Buddhist temples and in Siam where they were protected and treated with veneration in the Palaces and the Temples.

Through ancient Egyptian and Roman times Cats were used to protect stores of grain and other vulnerable food stocks, as indeed they are today.

It is remarkable that the Cat is not referred to in the Bible. It was around 1000 years ago in Britain when the domestic cat was given official recognition by the Welsh King Howel Dha when, it is alleged, he fixed a penny as the value of a kitten and twopence as the value of a cat which had caught its first mouse. A very high value indeed when related to today's values.

The penalty for killing a Cat was high indeed.

Britain was probably the last place in Europe into which the Cat was introduced as a domestic animal.

The migration of Cats almost certainly stemmed from Libia into Egypt from whence the Abyssinian, Chinchilla, Maltese, Persian and Tortoiseshell varieties all originated.

The Abyssinian cat supposedly descended from the Cats of Egypt is probably the nearest in general appearance to the distinctive breeds from Asia such as the Burmese and Siamese have in their independence of spirit and the markedly slim limbs and slender tail.

THE MOGGY or MOGGIE The name derived from the word mongrel loosely applied to all domestic cats of no particular breed or of mixed breed. The same term, 'mongrel', is also applied to dogs. Today the term 'feral' is loosely and inaccurately applied to any domestic cat which has gone wild, seemingly distinguishing it from the true Wild Cat.

TABBY As already stated cats were first commonest in the Middle East and in Egypt a thousand years before Christ, but it was not until the Byzantium period that a rich silk cloth with a watered or wavy pattern came to be manufactured in the areas around Persia, Syria and Iraq.

The Arabic for this cloth was 'attābī' originating because it was made at Al-'attābīya, a suburb of Baghdad, after the Prince Attāb who resided there.

Because of the pattern and the weave and the colouring cats with similar markings came to be called 'tabbīs' from which has derived our 'Tabby'.

BRINDLED The use of the description or title 'brindle' should not be confused with or used as an alternative description of a 'tabby'.

'Brindled' refers to or describes a much lighter mixture of light browns similar to that found in lions with streaks of grey and odd dark spots of an uneven pattern.

THE CAT-TIONARY

AILUROPHILE A cat lover or fancier.

AILUROPHOBE A person with an abnormal fear of cats. A cat hater.

CAT A domesticated or wild carnivore of the genus felis.

CATAMOUNT Term used in the United States to describe the cougar or puma.

CATAMOUNTAIN or CAT o'MOUNTAIN North American term for leopard, panther or ocelot.

CAT-BIRD An American bird of the thrush family called so because its note resembles the mewing of a cat.

CAT-CALL A form of whistle used by audiences to express their displeasure or annoyance with a performance. So called because it is a similar noise to that of cats 'catawauling'.

CATAWAULING The noise made by cats when in dissension with one another or prior to mating.

CAT'S CRADLE A game played by children with an intertwined cord around one another's fingers at the same time maintaining a symmetrical figure. (Origin of term so used unknown.)

CAT-EYED Having eyes like a cat: being able to see in the dark.

CAT'S FOOT A plant (common name Ground Ivy) so called because cats seem to like walking upon it.

CAT GUT A form of cord made from the intestines of animals, usually used as strings for musical instruments, clocks, etc. Usually sheep but *never* cats. It is strange it should have been so called except that the sound badly produced resembles a cat's wauling. More likely originating from the corruption of 'kit-gut', kit being an ancient word for a small fiddle.

CAT-HAMMED With thin hams like a cat.

CATHEAD A beam projecting from a ship's bows to which the anchor is secured. So called because the ring to which the anchor was drawn usually hung from an ornament commonly called a 'Cat's head'.

CATBRAIN Having a small brain like a cat.

CAT BURGLAR A burglar stealthy as a cat.

CAT HOLE(S) The two holes in the after part of a ship through which hawsers pass for steadying the ship. (So called because rats use hawsers for access to ship and the ship's cat awaits within the ship for them.)

CATHOOD State of being a cat or having the nature of a cat.

CAT FISH (Catfish) Any of numerous scaleless, chiefly freshwater fishes of the order Siluriformes characteristically having whisker-like barbels extending from the upper jaw similar to those of a cat.

CATS BRAINS Sandstone veined with chalk. An unpleasant reference used in geological circles to the 'nothingness' of such a combination.

CAT To vomit and also to raise the anchor to the Cathead, the former referring to the frequency with which cats tend to vomit.

CATS EYES Circular frosted glass used for road markings so called because of its similarity to the eyes of a cat at night. Also, any of various semi-precious stones displaying a band of reflected light that shifts position as the gem is turned, being a reference to the movement of a cats eye.

CAT LIKE Noiseless, stealthy.

CATLING A little cat, a kitten. Also a downy moss on some trees like the fur of a cat.

CATMINT Aromatic labiate plant with pale-blue flowers said to be so called because of the fondness of cats for it to use as a bed.

CAT-ICE Very thin ice from under which the water has receded and which would not bear the weight of a cat.

CATS WHISKER The very fine wire used in crystal wireless receivers about 80 years ago. Something very fine.

CAT SILVER A variety of silvery mica (again a reference to its reflective qualities similar to those of a cat's eyes).

CATS PAW A dupe used as a tool (an allusion to the fable of the monkey who used the cat's paw to pick chestnuts out of the fire). A light breeze (again a reference to the softness and delicacy of the touch of a cats paw).

CAT WITTED Small minded, conceited, spiteful. An unfair reference to cats intelligence and nature likely to arouse indignation in cat lovers.

CAT AND MOUSE ACT The Prisoners Temporary Discharge for Ill health Act of 1913 enabling suffragette hunger strikers to be released temporarily until they were recovered enough to be rearrested and imprisoned. (Obviously a reference to the behaviour of a cats treatment of a mouse when captured.)

CAT BEAM The broadest beam in a ship. The place where the ships cat used to sleep for safety.

CAT STICK A game and also the stick used in playing the game.

CATTED AND FISHED Expression used to describe an anchor which has been raised to the cathead and secured.

CAT o NINE TAILS Whip of 9 knotted cords formerly used in military and naval punishments. Probably so called because it scratches the back as a cat might.

CAT LICK A perfunctory treatment when washing. Performed carelessly or without interest. A careless wash or dust.

CAT NAP A short light sleep. A state of being only half asleep as with a cat.

CAT LADDER A kind of ladder used on sloping roofs.

CAT SALT Finely granulated common salt.

CAT SIX A double tripod with six legs so arranged it stands firmly on three legs (presumably originating from the ability of cats to remain on their feet).

CAT LAP Stuff fit for a cat to lap. Also, a contemptuous name for any non-alcoholic drink a cat would swallow.

CATTISH/CATTY Spiteful. Of or like a cat's nature. (Again a reference which would be hotly disputed by any cat lover.)

CATTERY A place where cats are bred or cared for in their owner's absence.

CAT FLAP A small inset in a wall or door permitting a cat entry or exit.

CAT WALK A narrow footway as above stage in a theatre or for fashion models. So called because cats tend to use narrow walk ways.

PUSS A common form of address used in various languages throughout Europe as a call-name for cats. In the 17th century it began to be used as a reference to hares. Mainly traceable to Teutonic origins its exact origin is unknown. The French misrepresentation of the Latin (lepus) meaning a hare into Le Pus is an amusing twist. (See also Pasht or Pusht.)

PUSS IN BOOTS Is the anglicisation of the French Nursery tale 'Le Chat Botte' from Straparola's 'Nights' (1530). For full story see 'Dick Whittington's Cat' (page 124.)

PASHT The name given to their Cat Goddess by the Egyptians. Less commonly known as … BUBASTIS the Greek name of Bast or Pasht, the Diana of Egyptian Mythology; she was daughter of Isis and sister of Horus, and her sacred animal was the CAT. (See also Adages 'From the Classics'.) LIVES

ADAGES, APHORISMS AND APOTHEGMS

A CAT HAS NINE LIVES The cat's natural instinct for survival both when in the wild and when domesticated, is no doubt the reason for this saying particularly its ability to land safely on its feet when falling.

A CAT MAY LOOK AT A KING Many origins have been suggested for this saying some dating as far back as the Egyptians when cats were venerated, roamed the palaces and sat beside or before the King.

A modern interpretation of the saying might be 'I am as good as you'.

ALL CATS LOVE FISH BUT FEAR TO WET THEIR PAWS Common knowledge has it that cats do not like to wet their paws and may even 'pass up' an opportunity to obtain fish rather than do so.

Modern interpretation: Someone who will not take the trouble or be put to the inconvenience or take the risk of getting what they want.

BEFORE THE CAT CAN LICK HER EAR As no cat is able to lick its ear this means 'never'.

CARE KILLED THE CAT A cat, too carefully looked after can be weakened despite its nine lives. A cat will survive without the help of others.

GRIN LIKE A CHESHIRE CAT A cat famous for grinning like the one in Lewis Carrol's 'Alice's Adventures in Wonderland'.

'Please would you tell me,' said Alice a little timidly, 'Why your cat grins like that?' 'It's a Cheshire cat,' said the Duchess, 'and that's why'.

Now used to describe someone who when smiling show their teeth and gums or someone who keeps smiling for no apparent reason.

ENOUGH TO MAKE A CAT SPEAK Said of something (usually liquor) that will loosen one's tongue.

'Come on your ways; open your mouth there is that which will give language to your cat, open your mouth.' Shakespeare: The Tempest

HANG ME IN A BOTTLE LIKE A CAT 'Hang me in a bottle like a cat' (from Much Ado about Nothing) Shakespeare.

In olden times a cat was, for sport, tied into a leather bottle or bag hung on a branch of a tree and used as a target for bowmen to shoot at. Also Percy mentions a variant of this 'sport' in his 'Reliques of Ancient English Poetry' (1765).

'It is still a diversion in Scotland to hang up a cat in a firkin and then the horsemen demonstrated their dexterity by opening the bags' bottom with a sword and escaping before the contents fell upon them.'

IN THE DARK ALL CATS ARE GREY Not until things come out into the open are their true colours and/or meaning distinguishable.

Also: All persons are undistinguished till they have made a name.

ITS RAINING CATS AND DOGS The phrase was coined by Jonathan Swift of Gulliver's Travels fame during lifetime of 1667–1745 in his writing 'Polite Conversation'.

'I know Sir John would go though he was sure it would rain cats and dogs.'

TO FIGHT LIKE KILKENNY CATS Generally accepted meaning to fight until both sides are exhausted or have nothing left.

Traditional interpretation: During the Irish rebellion of 1798 Kilkenny was garrisoned by a troop of Hessian soldiers, who amused themselves by tying two cats together by their tails and throwing them across a line to fight.

The authorities tried to stop the 'sport' but when Officers arrived a trooper cut the tails, the cats made off. When the Officer enquired 'what are these tails?' he was told two cats had been fighting and devoured each other but the tails.

TO LET THE CAT OUT OF THE BAG To disclose a secret. It was in early times a trick amongst country folk to substitute a cat for a sucking-pig and bring it in a bag to market. A greenhorn would buy the 'pig' without examination (buying a 'pig in a poke') but if a purchaser opened the sack he 'let the cat out of the bag'.

From Meredith 'The egotist' … 'She let the cat out of her bag of verse … she almost proposed to her hero in rhyme'

LIKE A CAT ON A HOT TIN ROOF OR 'ON BRICKS' Uneasy, restless, anxious to 'get way'. The phrase made famous by the film.

MUFFLED CATS CATCH NO MICE Said of those who work in gloves for fear of soiling their hands.

NOT ROOM TO SWING A CAT Swinging cats as a mark for sportsmen was once a favourite amusement.

The 'torture' of cats as various forms of amusement by the ignorant is alleged to have arisen through the cats supposed connection with witches and the occult.

See Dickens's reference in David Copperfield.

Much more likely is the mispronunciation of the word 'cot' amongst sailors when referring to a 'hammock' on board a ship in very cramped conditions 'Not room to raise a hammock'.

SEE HOW THE CAT JUMPS An alternative expression of 'see which way the wind blows' … or 'wait and see what happens'. Another interpretation may be reference to the game called 'tip-cat', in which the player has to observe which way the 'cat' has jumped.

SICK AS A CAT Here again it is related to the turning of a phrase by sailors when drinking. 'Cat' being used in many ways by sailors. In this case 'cat' is to vomit like a cat.

LIVING A CAT AND DOG LIFE A state of constant quarrelling and snarling.

'There will be jealousies and a cat and dog life worse than ever.' Carlyle: 'Frederick the Great'.

TO TURN CAT IN PAN The modern acceptance of the phrase is for it to mean to 'turn traitor' or to be a 'turncoat'. But the origins are disputed by such eminent philologists as Bacon and Johnson so any attempts to explain may well lead to confusion and indecision.

Nevertheless the French 'tourner côte en peine' when mutilated by English pronunciation became 'cat in pan' (to turn sides in trouble), and Bacon's pithy reference in his 'Essays of Cunning' is worth noting … 'There is a cunning which we in England call the turning of the "cat in the pan" which is, when that which a man says to another he lays it as if another had said it to him."

TOUGH NOT A CAT BUT A GLOVE The motto of the Mackintosh clan whose crest is 'a cat-a-mountain salient guardant proper', with, for supporters, 'Two cats proper'. 'Glove' here stands for a 'glaive', the old Scottish broadsword. Modern interpretation: 'keep away unless you want trouble'.

WHAT CAN YOU HAVE OF A CAT BUT HER SKIN? Reference to the skin of a cat which is the only useful part of it. Modern interpretation 'it has only one use'. Cats skins were once used for trimming coats and hats.

WHEN THE CATS AWAY THE MICE WILL PLAY This is a saying or proverb found in many languages back into time, all with the same meaning. Generally interpreted as meaning when the person(s) in authority are absent the lower echelons will misbehave, or fail to get on with their work.

CAT'S FOOT EXPERIENCE To live as a mouse under a cat's paw. To be at the whim of a cat's pleasure whether you live or die.

SOMETHING THE CAT BROUGHT IN 'Trophies' brought into the house by a cat are usually mutilated and damaged. Modern reference to someone wearing old and bedraggled clothing and looking untidy.

ENOUGH TO MAKE A CAT LAUGH Something sufficiently amusing to make the most unlikely person laugh. A reference to cats inability to appear pleased by facial expression.

NOT HAVE A CAT IN HELL'S CHANCE To have no chance at all.

PUT THE CAT AMONG THE PIGEONS To create a furore. To introduce a disturbing factor into a situation.

ITS THE CAT'S PYJAMAS OR WHISKERS The very thing which is wanted, the ideal thing, anything very good, or very sensitive.

PUSSY FOOTING To move stealthily; to act timidly or with excessive caution.

CAT A 'familiar' so called from the mediaeval superstition that Satan's favourite form was a black cat. Hence witches were said to have a cat as their familiar. The superstition may have arisen from the classical legend of Galinthias (qv) who was turned into a cat and became a priestess of Hecate.

In ancient Rome the cat was a symbol of liberty. The goddess of Liberty was represented as holding a cup in one hand, a broken sceptre in the other, and with a cat lying at her feet. No animal is so great an enemy to all constraint as a cat.

In Egypt the cat was sacred to Isis, or the moon. It was held in great veneration, and was worshiped with great ceremony as a symbol of the moon, not only because it is more active after sunset, but from the dilation and contraction of its pupil symbolic of waxing and waning.

The goddess Bast (see Bubastis), representative of the life-giving solar heat, was portrayed as having the head of a cat, probably because that animal likes to bask in the sun.

Diodorus tells us that whoever killed a cat, even by accident, was by the Egyptians punished by death, and according to Egyptian tradition, Diana assumed the form of a cat, and thus excited the fury of the giants.

Sir Winston Churchill would never of course have admitted it, but what does this quotation from his 'Memories and Adventures' tell us?

'A DOG LOOKS UP TO A MAN
A CAT LOOKS DOWN ON A MAN,
BUT A PIG WILL LOOK YOU IN
THE EYE AND SEE HIS EQUAL'

Even great men pay tribute, if but reluctantly, to the cat!!

THE TRUE STORY OF DICK WHITTINGTON AND HIS CAT

DICK WHITTINGTON AND HIS CAT

As with so many stories told in the nursery the story of Dick Whittington and his Cat is a mixture of truth, fable and transmuted folk lore, perhaps deliberately created to serve as an amusing interesting and inspiring story for the young.

It is generally accepted that the story of Dick Whittington and his Cat and the influence of his Cat in persuading him to return to London to make his fortune is a nursery story and only that.

But, as with so much of Folk Lore, Nursery Tales, Fables and Proverbs there is also a grain of truth or a twist to the facts which provided the basis of the story familiar to us today.

Before proceeding further it makes an interesting deviation to study the story of PUSS IN BOOTS.

'Puss in Boots' is the anglicised version of a nursery tale called Le Chat Botté from Strapola's 'Nights' in which Constantine's cat procures his master a castle and also the King's heiress. In 1585 it was translated into French from the Italian under the title 'Les contes de ma Mére l'Oie' and in this form it reached England.

The story is a simple one …'clever cat secures fortune and a high born lady for his master who pretends to have a title but is really a penniless young peasant miller'.

Bearing this story in mind one of the most fascinating aspects of the Dick Whittington story is that so much of the basic detail of the nursery tale is unquestionably true of Dick Whittington's life.

There is little doubt that the twist to the Dick Whittington story which we know today was done for the benefit of nursery consumption but in this case it seems a pity for here we have a story where 'truth is stranger than fiction'.

One of the most remarkable features of the Puss in Boots/ Dick Whittington similarities is that the Puss in Boots story was written more than 100 years after Dick Whittington died and one is tempted to speculate at what period in time the simple accounts of a respected and important man was turned into a nursery story. Was it around 1600 when the French version of Straparola's 'Le Chat Botté reached this country?

Richard Whityngdon was born about 1358, son of Sir William de Whityngdon, Lord of the Manor of Pauntley in Gloucester. He was a younger son and thereby unprovided for so when arrangements were made between his father and Sir John Fitz-Warren a relative who was a London Merchant, 13 years old Dick had to walk there to take up his apprenticeship.

Dick Whittington (as we shall refer to him) was good at his work and in due course Sir John agreed to a marriage between him and his daughter. It is perhaps churlish but never the less worldly to suppose that this helped set him on the road to fortune. (Note the similarity of the story to 'Puss in Boots'.)

King Richard II was on the throne and in 1397 the King recommended that Richard Whittington, who was then only 26 should become Lord Mayor of London. There was no doubt some political wisdom in this for the previous decade had been a period of civil unrest culminating in the death of Wat Tyler during a riot in Smithfield when he was slain by the previous Lord Mayor.

The riots, which had begun in 1381, because of the imposition of a Poll Tax to defray expenses of a war with France, were still going on and no doubt the presence of a new Mayor would be considered a calming influence.

Unfortunately for Dick Whittington King Richard II was forced to abdicate less than 2 years after he had made Dick Mayor and Henry of Lancaster became King.

Dick Whittington had continued to prosper since arriving in London, much of his fortune being amassed from transporting coal from Newcastle to London. The ship he used to this purpose was of Norwegian design with a flat bottom, a narrow stern, a deep waist and projecting quarters, the colloquial term used to describe the vessel being a 'Cat'.

It would not be unreasonable to suppose and there are no records to prove it either way, that Dick Whittington became apprehensive at the deposition of Richard II having been favoured of him and decided to leave London and go North to Newcastle where he could continue his coal trading safely out of the reach of Henry IV.

His early mentor Sir John Fitz-Warren had by then died and there was only his wife, who may very well have been with him at Highgate, when while resting he heard the Bells of Bow.

Perhaps the sound of the Bells of Bow and the good life which they signified was too much for him and the thought of the business he had with his 'Cats' influenced his return to London.

Fortunately for Dick Whittington, on coming to the throne, Henry IV found the Royal Coffers sadly impoverished and Dick was able to lend (a polite word in such circumstances for 'give') the King £1000 (probably in the region of £500,000 in todays values) thereby buying himself into the favour of the King.

Dick Whittington had to wait seven anxious years till 1406 before he again became Lord Mayor of London but in the mean time he had become even richer and more influential.

Seven years later in 1413, King Henry IV died and was succeeded by his eldest son who became Henry V. It seems that having loaned money to King Henry IV he had created a precedent for before long he was lending money to King Henry V.

By this time Dick Whittington was a mature 55 and had established certain benefactions to be administered after his death.

In 1419 Dick Whittington again became Lord Mayor of London and was knighted by the King. He had had to wait 40 years for recognition of his success and his good works.

Once again and only a year after having been Mayor he was attending the funeral of another King. King Henry V had died to be succeeded by his only son Henry VI.

Sir Richard Whittington died only a year after the new King had come to the throne, and presumably before the King had an opportunity of asking him for money as his predecessors had done!

Sir Richard had been an extremely popular and respected member of Society and has been styled 'the model merchant of the Middle Ages', a title justly earned long before the inspiring 'Puss in Boots' nursery story reached England.

Some historians attribute the story of Dick Whittington's cat to a confusion between the original French 'achat' meaning purchase or trade and the mispronunciation of the word by the English as 'a cat'.

It seems appropriate to end this account of Dick Whittington and his cat with the epitaph destroyed during the fire of London …

> 'Beneath this stone lies Wittington
> Sir Richard rightly named.
> Who three times Lord Mayor served in London,
> in which he ne'er was blamed.
> He rose from indigence to wealth
> By industry and that,
> For lo! he scorned to gain by stealth
> What he got by a cat!'

The cynical amongst us will no doubt ponder on the necessity of making huge bequests to the Crown if all one needs is a cat!

The haunted house (see page 19)

‘TIGGER’S TAIL’
A
SHORT STORY

'TIGGER'S TAIL'

Mrs Jones was found dead at 4pm on the 1st November 1985.

Mrs Jones was in her fading 80s; she lived in one of those Sheltered Housing apartments for old people who are still capable of caring for themselves with a Warden at hand.

The Doctor who was called was in a hurry; there were other more important cases needing his attention. He vaguely noticed that the place was very cold. His examination of the body showed nothing unusual. So far as he could determine Mrs Jones had just died. He could of course recommend a post-mortem, but his previous examinations of this dear old lady had indicated that for her age she was pretty fit except for a mild heart condition. So, it was 'cardiac arrest accelerated by hypothermia' which found its way on to the death certificate.

That November was particularly cold for the time of year and that might have been the end of it.

Mrs Jones would have died forgotten.

But it was no marching, banner waving, protesting do-gooder fighting the cause of neglected old age pensioners and the aged who brought Mrs Jones into the limelight but her cat.

At one time Mrs Jones had gathered around her quite a number of cats. She had loved them all. She had cared for them, sometimes to the detriment of her health, by feeding them rather than herself. She was a dear, harmless old lady who like quite a lot of other people irrespective of age, find comfort, solace and a greater sense of communion with their cats than with the humans around them.

And then someone in the Sheltered Housing, with nothing better to do and who was quite unaffected by the number of cats cared for by Mrs Jones had reported her to the authorities.

The 'Authorities' … no one knew who … probably someone in the form of a rolled-up shirt sleeved little hen-pecked male clerk or a thin lipped spinster wearing pince-nez with a too tight nose rest had rushed to the book of rules and discovered that one cat only, and *that* was a special concession, was allowed.

All this had happened a year earlier and when I started to make enquiries about the events prior to Mrs Jones' death I discovered her neighbours nodding knowingly and saying 'Oh! yes, when she lost her cats she began to decline … no doubt about *that* …' and lips were pursed and glances given which were supposed to tell a great deal but only contrived to make one realise how all those dear old people were desperately in need of interest in their limited lives.

Mrs Jones was obliged to make a decision. Which of the eight cats she was presently housing should she keep? She was always careful to see that all her cats had been 'attended to' as she liked to call it. Male or female it mattered not. They were tabbies, blacks, gingers, black and whites and no one knew where the beautiful long haired smokey persian had come from.

Someone, it seemed, had had compassion in the Citadel of the Authorities and given Mrs Jones two weeks to make up her mind which cat she wished to keep. For two whole weeks she agonised, and on the day a sympathetic RSPCA Inspector called with his little van to collect the offending seven she had still not made up her mind.

Gently Mr Thomas, the RSPCA man, explained that 'you really must make up your mind Mrs Jones and then, in panic Mrs Jones had said, pointing, 'him, I'll keep *him*'. 'Him' as I subsequently came to discover was a huge beautifully marked tabby with two of the largest most beautiful and appealing eyes ever seen in any animal. Mrs Jones had named him 'Tigger'. Obviously Tigger had just looked at her.

You may wonder how I came to be involved in all this …

I too am a cat lover. When I moved into the district I decided I would have myself a cat. That for a start, is a miss-statement for it is cats who choose you, not you cats. And so when I visited the RSPCA Cats' Home I had no choice but to have Tigger. As I walked through the cages there was Tigger sitting upright with great authority, looking at me with those beautiful appealing eyes, demanding my attention. I didn't hesitate and like Mrs Jones said 'him, I'll have him'.

I had taken along a wicker basket for my cat. The RSPCA attendant handed me Tigger out of the cage and as I took him into my arms he bit me. Not hard but a quite definite nip which I felt sure was merely to establish the relationship between us which I subsequently came to accept as being one of equals.

I asked the Inspector as I paid for him, where he had come from. Did he know Tigger's past history? It was then that I heard about Mrs Jones dilemma which I have just recounted.

Apparently it had not been long after the 'magnificent seven' had been collected, as the RSPCA Authorities had come to call the rescued cats, that Mrs Jones had died, and then it was a matter of collecting Tigger and finding a place for him too in the Cats' Home.

From the beginning Tigger and I had a very special relationship. There had been cats in my life for as long as I could remember and whilst some had been special cats whom I still remembered for their special characteristics others had been 'cats'.

Tigger, I soon realised, was different. In fact Tigger was *very* different.

Tigger emerged from his carrier with great dignity, rather like a Monarch stepping from the Royal Coach. I had opened the carrier in the kitchen where there was one of those leather covered high stools which one uses whilst waiting for the three minute egg.

Without hesitation Tigger jumped up on to the stool and sat there, emanating overpowering command. From that day the stool became Tigger's throne and no one was permitted to use it but him.

'Kitchen time' as Tigger and I came to call it was one of his greatest delights for he would sit on his haunches on the stool and as one passed, a paw would flash out complete with claws and one's hand would be drawn to his mouth where he would give a gentle nip a lick and a nuzzle. From the stool he received 'tid-bits' and from the stool he commanded attention.

Tigger tolerated his head being stroked but hated anyone touching his back. Anyone attempting to stroke him would receive a vicious bite or a quick flick from a paw with claws extended.

Tigger's marking was perfect. I have never seen such symmetry, such rich golden brown and black shading. His coat shone and the markings which came from around the 'collar' were just like a mayoral chain whilst the streaks which came evenly over his head were similar in shape to those on a cobra's hood.

Tigger was one of the most powerful most muscular cats I have ever had the privilege of meeting. Tigger was unlike the big cats such as Tigers and Lions who are lithe with powerful shoulder muscles. Tigger was built more like a bull dog, with a broad chest and whilst his body was big, solid and muscular he had slim rather prissy legs surmounted by the most delicate paws.

Tigger's most endearing feature was his pink nose which seemed incongruous with the rest of his appearance and his aggressive nature.

And then there was his tail. My cat loving friends whom I introduced to Tigger all declared they had never seen another cat with a tail like Tigger's.

I have said he was a big cat, and when I say that I *mean* big. But like his legs and his paws his tail seemed not to belong to him. It was too small. I had never seen a tail like it on any other creature. It was slim, short and powerful and rarely at rest. Almost all the time at least two inches of it was twitching and moving and when angry, annoyed or dissatisfied the 'thing' would quiver from top to bottom, the movement running in ripples from tip to base. It shivered and quivered like the stinging tail of a scorpion.

When the rest of Tigger's body seemed relaxed and quiet his tail told what was going on in his mind. One of my friends refused to call it a tail and insisted upon calling it 'that evil thing'.

Much as I quickly came to respect and to love Tigger I must admit I had to agree with my friend. Tigger's tail *was* evil. Even when on his best behaviour Tigger's tail was not. It had a life of its own. As I watched him, fascinated, I sometimes wondered if it *was* just a tail but some evil spirit which had entered Tigger at some time in the past and then taken residence there, leaving him with no control over it.

I suppose we had been together for around six months before I began to suspect Tigger was a schizophrenic. The reason for his bad temper seemed to have little logical origin. If he wanted to be bad tempered he was and one walked a safe distance from him on those occasions. He seemed particularly to love ladies ankles and the prettier and slimmer the ankle the less could he resist a nip.

He terrified the other cats in the neighbourhood simply by approaching them in a menacing way stepping daintily on his prissy paws and staring at them. They didn't stop to argue. I can't remember ever seeing him in a fight. He bullied by menace.

Yet there was little independence of spirit in Tigger for he followed me everywhere. He stayed in the bathroom when I was bathing or shaving and when I had finished waited for me to run freshwater into the handbasin for him to drink. If I used the WC he sat outside waiting for me to emerge.

Wherever I was garden, or house, bedroom, or kitchen there was Tigger. He desperately needed human company … that was evident. How much of Tigger's aggressive bullying was bravado I wondered? Did it hide a timid loving nature? Or was … he like some humans, afraid to be alone in case some quirk in their nature took possession of them?

I discussed my theories with a very good friend who was not so cat crazy as myself, she looked at me incredulously as I talked and when I stopped, it seemed an age before she said, 'Peter, you really must get this thing into perspective – it *is only* a cat you know'. She left soon afterwards making her excuses and I wasn't sorry to see her go. Her emphasis on the words 'is only' convinced me she and I had no future together.

It was six months before I became aware of one particular thing about Tigger … at the full moon his nature changed.

I can guess what you are thinking, because I thought the same thing … only black cats have a covenant with witches. It couldn't happen to a tabby, most people will say. But then, few people are aware that a certain line of tabbies was once always to be found wherever there was a coven of Sorcerers, and *this* puts tabbies above black cats in the hierarchy.

Everyone knows that a black cat without the saving grace of a few white hairs on its chest is still committed to the Community of Witches but not everyone knows how to detect which tabbies are still committed to the Sorcerer's Coven.

Whilst not believing nor practising Black Magic I have always been interested so I went to the library and there, sure enough in a book on Black Magic I found what I was looking for, a detailed explanation and a diagram of the markings of those tabbies still within the Circle of Sorcerers. The marking diagram showed that a pure tabbie has a letter 'M' on his forehead; a brand placed there by Merlin himself as the Chief Sorcerer ages and ages ago. I rushed home to examine very carefully Tigger's markings dreading what I might find.

As I entered the door Tigger was there as usual, sitting on his throne as dignified as ever welcoming me with those funny 'yak yak' noises which had no connection with a 'meow' and which were a kind of protest noise at being left alone for so long. Never had I heard Tigger 'meow' as cats are supposed to do. As I approached to examine his forehead he stood on his haunches, put up both front paws taking my hand between them and drew them to his mouth where he nipped and licked my thumb and fingers. He started to purr.

His purr was a loud rumbling thunder within his chest, the loudest purr I have ever heard from a cat. After a while he let go my hand satisfied with my response to his demonstration, and allowed me to hold the diagram I had made in the library alongside of his head. Yes … there it was … quite distinctly the 'M' for Merlin.

One of Tigger's most fascinating behaviour patterns was his habit of looking one straight in the eye and if not spoken to, jerking his head and whole body forward towards one without taking his eyes from yours and at the same time making a throaty gurgle. He seemed desperately wanting to speak.

After finding his 'M' markings I began making excuses for his fits of bad temper blaming them on the frustrations suffered by a high intelligence unable to communicate.

Human beings with afflictions making them unable to speak their thoughts and express feelings sometimes follow a similar pattern of body language.

There was no question that from being the most loving, dependent appreciative cat Tigger could, in a flash, become an angry cat with teeth, claws and a lashing tail. A bundle of malignity and threatening violence that frightened me and others who met him in those moods.

His tail would quiver and his whole powerful body would be a mass of tightly sprung muscle, his ears would lie back and his eyes get bigger holding ones own like a basilisk.

I had noticed that it was around full moon that Tigger was more prone to these attacks. I have called them 'attacks' but they were really a change of character.

Whatever the cause … they happened … I got used to them and I like to think our close relationship softened his attitude towards me whatever he was feeling on these occasions.

In contrast there were the times when he behaved in the enchanting and loving way ordinary cats will do. We played together with bits of paper folded into spills but most of all he loved his feather.

I would hold the feather high above him, let it go and as it twisted and turned in its fall he would watch until it came within catching distance. When he would rise on his haunches and take it in both paws.

If I was too busy to play with him then he would go to the table on which his paper spills were kept, knock it off and throw it up into the air himself catching and teasing it as he would a bird.

Eleven pm was Tigger's bedtime but this was always preceded by a period of playtime, once over he would first wait at the bottom of the stairs, waiting to see me move. When I did so he would rush to the top and sit waiting making his funny little 'yak yak' noises.

He slept in a large cardboard box lined with a blanket outside my bedroom door. Once I had retired he would be asleep and when he slept he snored as loudly as any old man after a heavy lunch.

Increasingly I found myself talking to him as if he were a human. We had developed a great rapport. We needed one another.

I am not superstitious nor am I easily frightened and I do not believe in Black Magic but I had been to the Library to read about it.

Then the day arrived when I wondered if I would not have to change my ideas.

It was around ten to eleven months since I had taken Tigger home from the RSPCA and now the date was October 31st … Halloween … as I later remembered.

No one had invited me to a party and no group of children had banged on the door saying 'trick or treat', to remind me of the fact. It happened to be a full moon at the same time as Halloween and Tigger was in one of his usual 'full moon moods' as I used to call them.

I had gone to bed at our usual time. I had read for a bit and before turning over for sleep had heard Tigger snoring away as usual.

It seemed only minutes before I was awakened by the most frightening noise. The noise came from outside the bedroom door. It was loud and powerful and sounded like the 'hiss' of a big tiger, and there was a tearing sound.

In the flash of understanding which comes to one in moments of stress I realised it could not be another cat in the house because I had closed all doors and windows before coming to bed.

I switched on the bedside light, got out of bed and opened the door.

I have to admit I was really scared by what I saw and felt. It was cold and I could *smell* evil. There was Tigger facing me with front legs spread apart tearing at the carpet with his claws, his head was up and his ears laid right back. From his mouth came this unbelievable sound of hissing.

I could embellish the description by an imaginative memory and say his eyes were flaming red … they were not … but most certainly they were larger than I had ever seen them and had a look of evil I had never seen before.

The basilisk stare was there again.

Because it was so unnatural his tail was the most frightening thing of all, it was extended horizontally like a pointer dog's but was quivering and twitching as if it had a life of its own.

He seemed unable to control it.

I thought he was going to spring at me.

I grabbed the eiderdown and as I stepped forward to cover him the hisses increased. I flung the eiderdown over him closing it around him and spoke soothing words to him. Gradually I felt him relax and the smell and the feel of evil receded.

I continued to talk to him and after a while I heard him purring.

I looked at my watch. It was only I5 minutes past midnight.

I treated Tigger as a parent would a child who had had a dreadful nightmare. I broke my rule and took Tigger on to my bed for the rest of the night where he slept soundly.

The fact that his snores and the experience of that night kept me awake was of no matter.

The following morning I went first to the Library and took out some Black Magic books. Then I went to the RSPCA and asked if they could give me the address where Mrs Jones had lived. A twenty minute run in the car and I arrived at the address given me. It did not take long for me to find out from one of the residents the name and address of the Doctor who had attended her.

I had to wait until the following day for an interview with him. To begin with he seemed reluctant to talk and had difficulty in remembering the particular incident when he was called out. I felt that with such a practical man there would be no point in trying to explain the real purpose of my visit. There would be no point in trying to tell him his diagnosis of death had been wrong.

Eventually he became sufficiently interested to look up his records to see if there had been any scratches on Mrs Jones' face. There had been. He had put them down to hand spasms as she had clutched at her face. I said 'Were her eyes open?' He gave me a penetrating quick glance, paused and said 'Yes'. I said 'Did she appear frightened?' He said 'Perhaps … a little … perhaps as much surprised', and then added 'but sometimes this expression *does* appear on people's faces who suffer a heart attack'. I said 'What was the date of her death?' He replied 'October 31st'.

There was nothing more I could do. Mrs Jones was dead and buried. *That* chapter was closed.

I did not go straight home to Tigger. I could not immediately face him for I realised Mrs Jones had died of sheer fright and that Tigger had either attacked her, or she had, as the Doctor believed, scratched her own face, not as he had suggested but in fending off what she *thought* was going to be an attack.

I could, of course, have his tail cut off, if, as I believed, the evil was settled in his tail. But I felt that that might not be the answer either. It would certainly completely ruin Tigger's appearance and Tigger would never recover his dignity and I should never be forgiven.

I went home still unresolved to Tigger. He 'yak yaked' at me, sat on his throne, bit my hand, licked my fingers, lashed his tail and purred. All as if nothing had happened.

I sat up late that night with Tigger snoring away happily in his box, and read my Black Magic books. I came to the conclusion the situation could be contained by simply having plenty of garlic in the house over Halloween and during the full moon.

It is now five months gone and the idea has worked. Life with Tigger is quieter but it is not Tigger who now has the reputation of being peculiar but me, for my friends cannot understand, and there is certainly no point in trying to explain to them, why I refuse all invitations at the full moon and Halloween, and why the whole house stinks of garlic.

Author's Note: As the reader will have realised this story is an adaptation of the true story related to the Author by Claire (See page 65) and their subsequent experiences with Tigger.

TAILPIECE

So far, Mankind has failed to demean the eat by breeding grotesque and ugly forms and we do not yet have the equivalent in cats of the panting, snuffling bulldog nor those pitiful breeds of dog with ridiculous and unnaturally short legs such as the Daschund or the Basset Hound.

Nevertheless *I* do believe that attempts to create new breeds with artificially induced 'qualities' for the sake of 'showing' and subsequently profit or personal pride, are to be deplored in the cat world.

Cat lovers and owners should be ever vigilant for sadly over the past two decades a new and horrifying attitude towards the cat has gained universal popularity in the USA.

Absurdly there has grown a belief that cats should, for their own safety (fraus) be kept indoors. A string of excuses is presented by the American cat welfare organisations including protecting cats from disease, rabies (which is common in the USA in dogs but not in cats) and road deaths.

As far back as 1960 American breeder and writer about cats, Milan Greer, promoted the idea that cats should be kept indoors. No doubt influenced by the need to convince the public that only specially bred cats were of any importance and ignoring the real nature of the cat.

The fact that there were millions of cat owners who were not interested in special breeds but simply wanted a cat as a companion passed him by.

The idea fitted into the American obsession with hygiene, cleanliness and organised life with the least possible effort. The result today is that there are millions of miserable cats living in circumstances alien to their natural instincts, NEVER allowed out of doors, never allowed to catch a mouse, scamper up a tree, lie in a clump of catmint or enjoy the smell of the good clean air.

Where the Egyptians for a thousand years and the Medieval cultures of their times accepted the cat, for better or worse, for what it was, it seems it will be the Americans who will once again despoil one of the few free living species.

Because cats kept indoors must exercise their natural need to scratch at objects to keep their claws comfortable and in condition, in America it is now common practice for cat owners to have their cats declawed.

THIS BARBARIC, CRUEL PRACTICE MUST **NEVER** BE ALLOWED IN THIS COUNTRY.

Whilst it is currently not allowed in Britain and the British Veterinary Association and the Royal College of Veterinary surgeons declaim against it this does not mean that some greedy, self-seeking breeder, or someone who sees a business opportunity in promoting the idea will not attempt to popularise the idea in Britain.

Index